Disruptive Innovation and Digital Transformation

Disruptive Innovation and Digital Transformation

21st Century New Growth Engines

Marguerite L. Johnson

BEP

BUSINESS EXPERT PRESS

Leader in applied, concise business books

Disruptive Innovation and Digital Transformation: 21st Century New Growth Engines

Worldwide Rights to publish and to distribute, Business Expert Press, LLC, 2021.

Interior design by Exeter Premedia Services Private Ltd., Chennai, India

First published in 2021 by
Business Expert Press, LLC
222 East 46th Street, New York, NY 10017
www.businessexpertpress.com

ISBN-13: 978-1-95253-892-6 (paperback)
ISBN-13: 978-1-95253-893-3 (e-book)

Business Expert Press Service Systems and Innovations in Business and Society Collection

Collection ISSN: 2326-2664 (print)
Collection ISSN: 2326-2699 (electronic)

First edition: 2021

10 9 8 7 6 5 4 3 2 1

In honor of my deceased father, George E. Johnston, Sr., and my deceased father-in-law, Duffy Johnson, Jr.

What People Are Saying

Description

Disruptive Innovation and Digital Transformation: 21st Century New Growth Engines is for executive leadership, senior management, innovation catalysts, and digital marketing teams tasked with transforming businesses by accelerating growth through disruptive innovations and digital capabilities. It is a practical guide with concise insights for understanding the applications of disruptive innovation and how to iteratively apply them to projects and opportunities. It garners insights from the best minds across relevant disciplines—from its original theory and latest updates—to arrive at new insights on digital transformation.

The author evolves key approaches to disruptive innovation theory to reveal new digital applications and tells leaders what to look for– major categories of customers' expectations in an escalating pattern to understand in what context digital plus disruptive innovations must be aligned with consumer preferences, environments, and the jobs-to-be-done, which is modeled in a new theory, Disruptive Innovation Customers' Expectations (DICE).

DICE provides methods to use to lead digital disruption across products, services, and business models. DICE translates the vague parts of disruptive innovation by simplifying them down to what-to-do. DICE takes away the elusive nature of disruptive innovation by advising leaders: how to scan, to track, and to detect disruptions.

This book provides leaders with the right lenses to filter markets, giving order to complexity, and making disruptive innovation simpler.

Keywords

disruptive innovation; digital transformation; innovation management; platforms; business models; networked ecosystems; strategy; transformational leadership; business transformation; entrepreneurship; startups; open innovation; collaboration; marketing; Internet of Things (IoT); digital disruption; innovation ecosystems; and digital marketing

Contents

Acknowledgments

- To those cited in this book: *Thank you for sharing your work, research, and insights. No book exists in a vacuum.*
- To my editors: *a Special "Thank you" to Jim Spohrer, PhD, Director, Cognitive Opentech Group (COG, IBM Research) and to Scott Isenberg, Managing Executive Editor (Business Expert Press).*
- To Innovation Research Interchange (IRIweb.org), a member organization: *It is truly an honor to be on the Board of Directors (2019-2021).*
- To my amazing husband (Michael) and our beautiful children (Kayla and Kyle): *I love you. You bring joy into my life. Thank you for listening to me and allowing me to drag you through the depths of disruptive innovation theories and digital transformation business cases. No words can convey the feelings in my heart.*

Marguerite Johnson
Bloomfield Hills, MI, USA

Preface

This book is written for business leaders by an innovation leader who understands the pressures of *delivering* on new growth. These pressures have intensified in the face of massive shifts in digital technologies, platforms, products, services, and business models. Like most of you, I did not have the time to "deep-dive" into the innovation literature to find all of the answers I needed. Nevertheless, digital transformation does not care. The changes it brings are disruptive. It has Newton's first law of physics on its side. The law of gross tonnage: The heavier vessel always has the right-of-way.

For a business leader looking to apply knowledge from the literature on digital transformation and disruptive innovation, it takes a tremendous amount of time to dedicate to finding, sorting, sifting, reading, and analyzing. This is not helped by the "[m]any researchers, writers, and consultants who use 'disruptive innovation' to describe any situation in which an industry is shaken up and previously successful incumbents stumble. But that's much too broad a usage" (Christensen et al. 2015). So, I did the work of synthesizing past research to demonstrate a pattern of six disrupters, I coined "Pattern of Disruptions". These disrupters are a part of a larger theory and model, which I detail in Chapter One.

I reread many of the latest leading innovation books, articles, research studies, business cases, and industry reports on disruptive innovation, digital transformation, and digital disruption. I found the literature was insightful, but incomplete and vastly disjointed. You will find that I quote industry experts from these fields: disruptive innovation, digital transformation, business, strategy, and technology because I want readers to understand my perspectives do not exist in a vacuum. They are reinforced and shared across a community of leaders. There are entire books written on the chapters in this book. I did not attempt to capture all of the works that have been published on disruptive innovation and digital transformation. I extracted only the contextual meanings or significance from leading works. I took everything and viewed it through the lens of my

20-year career in business, innovation leadership, new product development, strategy, and product line (with P&L) management.

My passions for business, innovation, and strategy compelled me to write this book. I hope you find value in my methodologies, my new theory and model on disruptive innovation, and my synthesis of decades of research to equip business leaders with answers for the 21st-century. I hope they ignite the new growth engines of disruptive innovation and digital transformation in your organizations. Thomas M. Siebel, groundbreaking technology and business leader, has this advice in his book, *Digital Transformation: Survive and Thrive in an Era of Mass Extinction*: "In management, I find one of the most important skills is pattern recognition: the ability to sort through complexity to find basic truths you recognize from other situations" (2019). This book is the results of my work to identify patterns, sort through complexities, and reveal new insights into disruptive innovation and digital transformation. As the saying jokingly goes: *I took one for the team.*

PART I

It's the Background

INTRODUCTION

Digital Was Missed

Disruptive innovation and digital transformation are the two capabilities qualified to tackle the new growth challenges facing all companies in the 21st-century—regardless of size, industry, market, or sector. This statement best describes the current business environment. They collaboratively work together to power growth. The disruptive innovation approach informs what companies look for in order to accelerate growth. Digital transformation informs which mediums and how they are used to achieve growth. "If you don't understand disruptive innovation, your digital transformation efforts could all be for nothing" (Jefferies 2019). This book defines "disruptive innovation" as the process of creating new products, services, business models, and/or platforms that redefines customers' expectations, changes consumers' behaviors, and creates a new standard for customer value. The process involves customer intimacy, the detailed insights that come from understanding how a customer's needs translate into a customer's expectations. The work in this book evolves decades of research on disruptive innovation to prepare business leaders for new growth in the 21st-century. Digital plays a significant role in all future innovations, but it propels disruptive innovations in news ways—not before discussed.

This digital collaborative approach to disruptive innovation is a very different approach than most companies deploy today. "Much of today's innovation relies on the SIP [Structural Innovation Paradigm] that is focused on fulfilling customer needs with one goal in mind: delivering a product or service that is better, faster and cheaper than the customer can get from any competitor" (Simanis et al. 2009). Companies relying on the SIP approach to innovation have an intentional focus on maximizing their operating profits while simultaneously increasing the performances of their products. Their business operating models focus on increasing efficiencies and improving performance. However, in the 21st-century profitability—from these levers—has reached its limits. Consequently, accelerating along these paths will not generate the new growth companies need in the future.

The new growth engines of disruptive innovation and digital transformation are focused on effectiveness in creating customer value—not strictly on productivity gains. Companies will need a different set of levers for future profitable growth. They will need to engage with customers to understand where to innovate. This shifts away from the SIP innovation approach. This will be hardest for large enterprise companies that are built around legacy assets and operations. This book demonstrates how to engage customers of all types (current, latent, and future): current customers defined as engaged in brand loyalty and/or consuming products and services; latent customers defined as new consumers from existing markets with unmet needs or unrealized expectations; and future customers defined as nonconsumers who previously relied on disparate solutions or alternative substitutions to meet their needs. This book helps companies uncover disruptive innovations that can only be understood by tapping into customers' expectations and unlocking capabilities through digital transformation.

Why Is Digital So Significant?

In addition to a different approach to innovation, companies will need to understand and to accept that customers have access to complete information. In the digital future, customers can draw from a broad network of information and sources (Rogers 2016). Customers can act on that information to access and to purchase from a company's competitors, alternatives, and substitutions. No longer will companies have an information advantage over customers. The speed of developments in technology and science, the pace of change in innovation, and customers access to an abundance of information means companies cannot debate whether to focus only on strategic customers, fitting their operating model, or to innovate in new markets. They must do both.

The world has been evolving toward a digital future of connected devices for nearly 30 years. "According to research from Gartner, approximately 26 billion objects would be linked together in the [Internet of Things] IoT by 2020, 33 billion in laptops, PCs, and smartphones were added" (Collis 2018). Connectivity and data transfer for all of these devices were made possible nearly 47 years ago in 1973: "the U.S. Defense Advanced Research Projects Agency (DARPA) initiated a research program to investigate techniques and technologies for interlinking packet networks of various kinds" (Leiner et al. 2017). The standardizations (or communication protocols) that were developed allowed "networked computers to communicate transparently across multiple, linked packet networks" (Leiner et al. 2017). The result was the "Internetting project and the system of networks which emerged from the research was known as the 'Internet'" (Leiner et al. 2017). A host of other protocols followed: "TCP/IP Protocol Suite, after the two initial protocols developed: Transmission Control Protocol (TCP) and Internet Protocol (IP)" (Leiner, et al 2017), the "Netscape browser" enabled by Hypertext Markup Language (HTML), and universal resource locators (URLs) (Anthony et al. 2017). The end result was the start of digital information spreading.

Around 1986, a number of "backbone facilities" were created to transfer large packets of data between networks. This was critical infrastructure added by the U.S. National Science Foundation (NSF) NSF-NET, the National Aeronautics and Space Administration (NASA) NSINET, and the U.S. Department of Energy (DOE) ESNET (Leiner et al. 2017). "In Europe, major international backbones such as NOR-DUnet [NORDUnet is a network of 5 Nordic National Research and Education Networks] and others provide connectivity to over one hundred thousand computers on a large number of networks" (Leiner et al. 2017). In the 1990s, commercial Internet backbones emerged to transport packets. These backbones enabled networks to connect and to link together into a vast network of networks. The combined system is the modern-day Internet. It consists of networked networks of giant carriers. These networks are owned and operated by different companies. "The individual core networks are privately owned by Tier 1 Internet Service Providers (ISP) ... AT&T, CenturyLink, Cogent Communications, Deutsche Telekom, Global Telecom and Technology (GTT), NTT Communications, Sprint, Tata Communications, Telecom Italia Sparkle, Telia Carrier, and Verizon" (Greene 2020). The digital protocols,

Internet backbone infrastructure, network architecture, and carriers are a networked ecosystem that has been fueling digital innovations over the past 30-plus years (Webb 2019).

Notwithstanding, the Internet alone is insufficient to drive new technologies. "[E]ven the most astounding new technologies can fail to gain traction in the marketplace" (Johnson 2018). Consequently, companies with a command of innovation practices, processes, talent, products, and services, as well as supporting value propositions and business models, can navigate new growth through disruptive innovation and digital transformation.

Why Should Businesses Be Concerned?

Without the insights in this book, a business leader, who understood disruptive innovation based on past readings of Christensen's theory of disruption, could miss out on the impact of digital transformation on the future of innovation. Clayton Christensen's *Theory of Disruptive Innovation* (hereinafter referred to as "the original theory") began as a narrowly focused theory of B2B markets. Christensen's original theory defined disruptive innovation as a "phenomenon by which an innovation transforms an existing market or sector by introducing simplicity, convenience, accessibility, and affordability where complication and high cost have become the status quo—eventually completely redefining the industry" (Christensen 2016). It focused on transforming existing markets or sectors through innovations when entrants offered products and/or services at the low-end of the market (frequently through lower pricing) to customers of incumbent companies and then advance upmarket. Christensen did not address the abilities of incumbents to create new markets with an offensive strategy of disruptive innovation. He would later acknowledge this in a book he wrote in 2016 (Christensen et al. 2016). He primarily considered market creation as an outcome of entrants innovating in markets that incumbents ignored. Albeit narrow, the original theory offered the business community a way to describe a scenario—B2B markets shifting and disappearing as the result of innovative new products and services.

The original theory has had "a profound effect on academic literature and management mindset" (Reinhardt et al. 2011). Disruptive innovation has been extensively covered, which could make the phrase appear over-used. Despite the widespread use of the phrase, the books, and the many articles written about disruptive innovation, I struggled with the practical aspects of the theory to find new growth potential for the 21st-century. Consequently, I reread old books and read new books, articles, research studies, and industry reports that followed Christensen's work, search-ing for additional insights. I was able to detect several reasons to reopen the discussion on disruptive innovation—mainly around digital, which Christensen admitted to missing in his original theory—likely do to the timeframe when his original theory was published in 1997 (Christensen et al. 2015). Although the world's digital infrastructure was well under-way by then, the impact of digital would not demonstrate its full domi-nance until 2007. Thomas Friedman wrote about this inflection year in a chapter of his book, Thank you for Being Late, *What the Hell Happened in 2007?* (Friedman 2016).

Since his first published works, Christensen answered to critiques of his original theory in a 2015 *Harvard Business Review* article, "What Is Disruptive Innovation?" It covered the ways in which he modified his original theory. For instance, he clarified: "Entrants that prove disrup-tive begin by successfully targeting those overlooked segments, gaining a foothold by delivering more-suitable functionality—frequently at a lower price" (Christensen et al. 2015). He reinterprets the success of entrants, tying it to overlooked segments by incumbents. Later, in a 2020 interview with *MIT Sloan*, Christensen added technology as an enabler.

> Disruptive innovation describes a process by which a product or service powered by a technology enabler initially takes root in simple applications at the low end of a market—typically by being less expensive and more accessible—and then relentlessly moves upmarket, eventually displacing established competitors (Christensen 2020).

Fundamentally, Christensen alerted the world to a new phenomenon. His peers and industry leaders acknowledged his works, and fellow authors contributed to enhance and to advance his original theory. There have been several key subsequent theories that expanded upon

Christensen's original theory. One of those books was written in 2015, *Big Bang Disruption: Business Survival in the Age of Constant Innovation*, by Larry Downes and Paul Nunes. It evolved the original theory of disruption to alert companies about disruptions "increasing in quality" that move upmarket. Christensen agreed with this revision to his original theory. "Disruptive innovations don't catch on with mainstream customers until quality catches up to their standards" (Christensen et al. 2015). I shift the focus away from B2B markets and incumbents in Christensen's theory, centering the focus onto customers' expectations in my own theory, detailed later in Chapter One. I expand upon Downes' theory to include digital capabilities that reinforce quality through reliability of assets and security in my theory, as well.

There is a chapter in another book that significantly contributed to the original theory. It is "Chapter Seven: Mastering Disruptive Business Models" of *The Digital Transformation Playbook: Rethink Your Business for the Digital Age* by David Rogers (2016). Rogers introduced a new theory of disruptive innovation to address: "disruption that is driven by consumer purchase behaviors, disruption that starts with the incumbent's core customers (rather than starting with new markets), and disruption that is driven by values other than price or access" (2016). This is where Rogers agrees with Downes that disruptive innovation must create value beyond simplicity and accessibility, which were the basis of Christensen's theory. His theory of business model disruption is two-sided (value proposition and value network), focusing on existing markets:

- "A difference in the value proposition that dramatically displaces the value provided by the incumbent (at least for some customers)" (Rogers 2016).
- "A difference in value network that creates a barrier to imitations by the incumbent" (Rogers 2016). These networks involve "people, partners, assets, and processes that enable the business to create, deliver, and earn value from the value proposition" (Rogers 2016).

Rogers' insights on business model innovation started with identifying a flaw in the original theory of disruptive innovation—the definition of "customer." In the original theory, only B2B customers were included.

Rogers suspected this is what led Christensen to miss disrupters that were consumer-driven. "Its origins in B2B industries may be the reason Christensen's theory explains a great many cases of disruption but missed others" (Rogers 2016). Rogers refocused and directed his theory toward consumer purchase behaviors (value propositions). In doing this he was able to build onto the original theory of disruption for incumbents with business model innovation (value networks). "My intent is to use the business model specifically as a predictor of business disruption, and for this purpose, the schema can be simpler" (Rogers 2016). Rogers points out that "value networks" are areas where established companies are unwilling to change. "[T]he existing value network of the incumbent prevents it from imitating the appealing new offerings of its challenger" (Rogers 2016). The challengers' "value networks" do not replicate the assets or operating models of incumbents, which make incumbents uninterested in switching to the challengers' new operating models. This unwillingness to change value networks will adversely impact incumbents' innovation value propositions, as well.

Rogers' theory effectively identified two dimensions for disruptive innovation. I am grateful for Rogers' work. I incorporated Rogers' theory of a two-sided approach to disruptive innovation (without his narrower focus on "incumbent's core customers"). However, I highlight the shift in the value formula between dimension-one (products and services) and dimension-two (business models including digital platforms) over time. Most markets originate from a product or a service, thus value generation starts in dimension-one. As a result of digital, as time goes on more value is generated in dimension-two. This shift in value creation is important. It is the digital tipping point. Companies with products and services that have not been digitally transformed risk losing their leverage in the value creation formula. Also, I offer ways to reinterpret his use of the phrase "consumer purchase behaviors" for products with my theory's major categories of customers' expectations. Finally, I added a third dimension that needs to be monitored, the innovation S curve. This dimension reflects the maximum combined value creation of dimensions one and two, the saturation level.

Alongside others, Christensen contributed to modifying and to clarifying his original theory. Christensen coauthored a book, a companion theory to his original theory of disruptive innovation, to factor in customer behaviors. The title of that book is *Competing Against Luck: The*

Story of Innovation and Customer Choice (Christensen et al. 2016). In the mid-1990s, he realized his original theory did not answer "what a company should do offensively to be successful: if you do this and not that, you will win" (Christensen et al. 2016). He called this companion theory "Theory of Jobs to Be Done" (Christensen et al. 2016). This theory's contribution is near and dear to me because it was inspired by a conversation Christensen had with a Detroit consultant, Bob Moesta. (I was born and raised most of my childhood in the city of Detroit.) Later I reference this conversation and how it impacted Christensen's theory of "jobs to be done." I reinterpret and build upon Christensen's jobs theory by filling in some of its gaps, such as refining customer needs in the context of customer expectations and interpreting saturation of addressable needs.

What New Information Will This Book Offer?

Although there are many books that expanded upon Christensen's original theory, none of them synthesized it with other disruptive innovation theories to create one comprehensive theory. This book does that work, as well as expands upon the combined theories in these ways: it builds out the methodologies to track, to scan (monitor), and to detect disrupters; it defines disrupters in a pattern (escalating categories of customers' expectations) as the directional forces that guide and create opportunities for new value creation; and it identifies disrupters made possible through digital and business models.

The synthesized theory is called *Disruptive Innovation Customers' Expectations* (hereinafter referred to as *DICE*) *Theory*. It is a phenomenon of changing consumer purchase behaviors that starts with the initial introduction of a product or service, escalates through a pattern of major categories of customers' expectations (accessible, dependable, reliable, usable, delightful, and meaningfulness) that is driven by customers' adoption of new capabilities and new technologies, which ends in consumers' behaviors being redefined into a new set of customers' expectations. New value is created from products, services, business models, and/or merging existing customers with non-consumers around a new set of expectations resulting in new markets, new industries, or new sectors. Void of changing consumers' behaviors and redefining customers' expectations around a new set of customer value an innovation is not disruptive.

Throughout the book I build on elements and dimensions of the theory to demonstrate its application, using models and illustrations. In the following chapters I provide various examples to demonstrate when a disruptive innovation effectively disrupted a market, changing consumers' behaviors around a new set of customers' expectations for value creation. This is an important distinction to make in the practice of innovation. It is different than general innovations that increase sales, build brand loyalty, and compete well in the marketplace. General innovations have momentary impacts on customers' behaviors. They do not permanently change behaviors or redefine expectations for value creation. Acknowledging that general innovations can be popular without being disruptive can prevent companies from being blindsided. It also helps companies improve how they calculate risks to their investments and how much weight they put on innovations in their pipeline for strategic planning. Questioning, observing, networking, and experimenting can help leaders reveal the true nature of an innovation (Dyer et al. 2019).

Here is a brief history of the evolution of key published works on disruptive innovation that shaped my investigations:

You Are Here

2020

Lead and Disrupt book
O'Reilly III et al, 2016

Disruptive Innovation and Digital
Transformation book (2020)
Marguerite Johnson, 2020

The Digital Transformation Playbook
Rethink Your Business for the Digital Age
Rogers, 2016
Competing Against Luck book (Fall, 2016)
Christensen et al, 2016

"What's Disruptive Innovation article!" HBR (Winter, 2015)
Christensen et al, 2015

MIT Sloan In-Depth Case Study (Fall, 2015)
"How Useful Is the Theory of Disruptive Innovation?"

Big-Bang Disruption (2014)
Downes et al, 2014
The Innovator's Guide to Growth book (2006)
Anthony et al, 2006

The Innovator's Solution book (2003)
Christensen et al, 2003

The Innovator's Dilemma book (1997)
Christensen

"Disruptive Technologies Catching the Wave" HBR (1995)
Bower et al,1995

1995

Gray scale = published year

Figure I.1 Key published works on disruptive innovation (1995–2020)

Regrettably, Clayton Christensen passed away before I wrote this book. So, I will not have the benefit of hearing his thoughts on the ways I recommend evolving his original theory. I will pick up from where he and others left off because disruptions have increased enabled by digital and businesses continue to struggle to find new growth opportunities. My investigations and learning are captured in this book. It reassured me that the decades of coverage, since 1995 when Clayton Christensen first wrote about the theory in *Harvard Business Review*, is still relevant today.

How Is This Book Organized to Present a Comprehensive Approach to Disruptive Innovation?

1. Only the absolutely necessary information is included, supported by meaningful examples, case studies, tables, and illustrations; in order to fully comprehend the *DICE Theory* and the actionable guidance it suggests for business leaders, strategic planners, futurists, and customer experience digital marketers I suggest reading the entire book.
2. Chapters are portioned into parts to give the reader a sense of how the information "fits" into the overall book: It's the Background; It's the Framework; It's Mastery; and It's Control.
3. Each chapter is a self-contained comprehensive package of insights and information on the subject (only when necessary are cross-references used to direct the reader back to sections, figures/tables, or chapters to review for additional insights).

CHAPTER 1

The Origins of *Disruptive Innovation Customers' Expectations (DICE)* Theory

This book intends to demonstrate some aspects of disruptive innovation that have been overlooked in the past, possibly explained by the popularity of the original theory that ultimately left many questions unanswered and possibly explained by the timing of the original theory. It highlights some new observations about disruptive innovation, suggests ways that these new observations can be applied, and highlights new insights for businesses looking to undergo digital transformation. The *DICE Theory* targets new growth areas with precise navigation to future disruptions. Finally, it is a warning to innovation practitioners that there are massive disruptive innovations accelerated by digital technologies underway, and Christensen may have underestimated the impacts to any organization looking to survive digital disruption. The risks to incumbent companies are greater. They have less room for maneuverability than a new entrant.

This chapter is organized simply (who, what, when, why, and how) to provide readers with necessary building blocks to ground all other content in this book.

Who Is Impacted?

Creating new growth is the mandate for all leaders, and the job of creating new growth falls within the responsibilities of senior management. The original theory left companies with a few blind spots—not that they cannot be overcome, but if left unchecked they could mislead companies in the digital future. Disruptive innovation and digital transformation represents opportunities to grow in new areas for businesses with the right capabilities. However, it can be hard to identify those capabilities, using the original theory. Christensen admits that it is limited; others contributed to improve the original theory, but there are still gaps. "But the strategic model of disruptive innovation we've all become comfortable with has a blind spot" (Downes et al. 2015).

I already covered the broader scope of needs to revisit in the original theory for disruptive innovation and digital. In this section I detail my observations of key phenomena to refine and to refocus them. As follows I highlight four (4) main areas for leaders, areas where I revisited and reassessed when applying the original theory to growth in the 21st-century. This sheds light particularly for those who were previously exposed to the original theory or any of its past iterations. These areas should be revisited:

1. Christensen acknowledged that his original theory of disruptive innovation...

   doesn't predict or explain how, specifically, a company should innovate to undermine the established leaders or where to create new markets. It doesn't tell you how to avoid the frustration of hit-and-miss innovation—leaving your fate to luck. It doesn't tell you how to create products and services that customers will want to buy—and predict which new products will succeed. (Christensen et al. 2016)

   There was a study by *MIT Sloan*'s Andrew A. King and Baljir Baatartogtokh. They conducted an in-depth case study analysis of 77 disruptive innovation cases discussed in *The Innovator's Dilemma* and *The Innovator's Solution* "to understand how to apply the theory of disruptive innovation" based on four key elements focused on incumbents: "incumbents in a market are improving along a trajectory of sustaining innovation," "they overshoot customer needs," "they possess the capability to respond to disruptive threats," and "incumbents end up floundering as a result of the disruption" (King et al. 2015). The *MIT Sloan* team interviewed one or two experts from each case study. To control for bias, the *MIT* team allowed respondents to be anonymous. "Many of the theory's exemplary cases did not fit four of its key conditions and predictions well" (King et al. 2015). A small number of cases fit all four, for example, "the disruptions by Salesforce.com, Intuit's QuickBooks, and Amazon.com" (King et al. 2015). Noteworthy, Christensen recognized the theory's inability to perfectly explain all aspects of a dynamically changing environment and multifaceted decisions that led to disruptive innovations. "More nuanced case analysis, he argues, shows that the theory of disruptive innovation explains the failure of leading businesses, time after time and industry after industry" (King et al. 2015).

2. Christensen's original theory provided B2B incumbents with a defensive competitive strategy for their existing markets. Christensen admits that his theory is a "theory of competitive response to an innovation" (Christensen 2016). Christensen argued disruption opens up markets held by incumbents when entrants offer low-end goods to consumers or entrants offer increased functionality, most frequently with lower prices. This is one of the ways Christensen elaborated on the original theory to include "two types of markets that incumbents overlook": "low-end footholds" products that customers deem "good enough" and "new-market footholds, disrupters create a market where none existed" by "offering an affordable solution to individuals and small organizations—and a new market was created" (Christensen et al. 2015). Entrants progress upmarket expanding on their original footholds, thereby decreasing revenues of incumbents and denying them future growth opportunities. "When mainstream customers start adopting the entrants' offerings in volume, disruption has occurred" (Christensen et al. 2015).

3. The innovations of entrants were disruptive to incumbents. Incumbents reacted defensibly to entrants' innovations. W. Chan Kim and Renée Mauborgne defined the types of innovations Christensen prescribed for incumbent's defense in his original theory, as "value innovations," competitive strategies in their book *Blue Ocean Strategy* (2005). These types of innovations create "a better product or a new brand but not disruption" (Rogers 2016). Christensen did not study entrants as part of his original theory. Later, Christensen coauthored a book, *The Innovator's DNA*, which studied the behaviors of new entrant innovators: such as Amazon, eBay, and Tesla.

4. Lastly, the absence of a robust proactive innovation strategy for large incumbent companies in the original theory steered them toward a single type of disruptive innovation, business model innovation. Looking to one of the first market leaders to apply Christensen's original theory of disruptive innovation, we find Proctor & Gamble (P&G). In 2004, P&G's executive leadership tasked two 30-year veterans of P&G to design "a new-growth factory whose intellectual underpinnings would derive from the Harvard Business School professor Clayton Christensen's disruptive-innovation theory" (Brown et al. 2011). P&G codified its answer to disruptive innovation: "Disruptive—new brands or business models that win through simplicity or affordability" (Brown et al. 2011). This is competitive strategy, defensive maneuvering to protect incremental product innovations. A new business model singularly is not the answer to "disruptive-innovation theory" (Roger 2016). P&G was not alone in leveraging Christensen's theory of disruptive innovation as a tool to create new growth. "Many leaders of small, entrepreneurial companies praise it as their guiding star; so do many executives at large, well-established organizations, including Intel, Southern New Hampshire University, and Salesforce.com" (Christensen et al. 2015). P&G deserves immense industrywide respect for its courage to step up to the challenges it faced to grow. It is an established leader in innovation and a curator of remarkable brands. The goal of this book is not to shame or to discourage companies from facing down threats with whatever credible means they have in their defense arsenals. It is only to recognize that disruption is a dynamic challenge, and it needs the full "light of day" to understand it.

What Are the Observed Phenomena?

The phenomena that I observed clearly defines the original theory of disruptive innovation is a strategy for incumbents businesses to defend against competitors. It does not capture a wider lens of innovation outside of the perspectives of incumbents being disrupted by entrants in their existing markets. It does not address the need to find growth in new markets, when customers evolve beyond the original theory's assumptions of "simplicity, convenience, accessibility, and affordability." This is an important reason to look more closely at the innovation approaches of the past and to evaluate their continued effectiveness to meet the challenges of the future.

In a book by Rita McGrath, *Seeing Around Corners* (based on a concept developed by Andy Grove), she calls attention to an observation made by Grove—a strategic inflection point "is a time in the life of a business when its fundamentals are about to change" (McGrath 2019). The awareness of strategic inflection points must be maintained. Companies should formalize a process to continually horizon-scan for strong (near) and weak (farther) signals. Any company that neglects this work runs the risks of being blindsided by disruptive forces (Webb 2020). In order to move forward with our reset on the original theory, we must clear up a few other areas that could obstruct our way forward.

The *DICE theory* addresses all of the incongruences in the original theory that I observed, as well as it shines a light on other key phenomena that are not mentioned in the original theory, but they must be addressed in order to grow in the digital future. The capabilities of finding, identifying, and targeting new areas for growth are desperately needed. Like much of this book, the answer to finding, identifying, and targeting new growth for the digital future was the result of my work to aggregate knowledge, filter it through my lens as a business leader and an innovation practitioner, and bring in my observations, investigations, and research from other published works.

Let us start at "finding": Gartner describes an emerging technologies phenomenon in its *Hype Cycle* phases: Innovation Trigger, Peak of Inflated Expectations, Trough of Disillusionment, Slope of Enlightenment, and Plateau of Productivity, a downward slope develops between "Peak of Inflated Expectations" and "Trough of Disillusionment." I was left with these observations: (1) a need to improve upon the original theory to understand the multiple points of disruptions that are capable of avoiding the downward spiral in the *Hype Cycle*—from "Peak" to "Trough"—and (2) a suspicion that focusing on the customer was the best place to correct this pitfall. I argue that the downward slope is where companies' innovations and customers' expectations for value creation never caught up to one another to gain realignment. I also argue that companies fall into this "Trough" because they are not factoring in the results of customers considering other aspects after gaining access to an innovation. "One of the most consistent patterns in business is the failure of leading companies to stay at the top of their industries when technologies or markets change" (Bower et al. 1995).

Onto "identifying": Abraham Maslow's philosophy of human's basic needs (physiological, safety, love and belonging, esteem, self-actualization) does not equip companies with sufficiently detailed information to innovate. Companies should avoid tracking basic needs outside of the contexts of customers' expectations and consumer purchasing behaviors. It is important to note: building innovations off of a set of "universal" needs fails to acknowledge that everyone does not have the same expectations for how her/his needs are met nor when/if she/he will act on them with a purchase. There must be a method to consider customers' needs as an evolving loop—from customer expectations—to new value creation— to changed consumer purchase behaviors. Christensen cautioned leaders to avoid labeling a product or service as disruptive innovation, but instead apply his theory in an evolutionary way to understand an environment (Christensen et al. 2015).

Finally, "targeting", which iteratively systematizes the efforts for both "finding" and "identifying": patterns are excellent sources of evidence. Pattern recognition is an established methodology used in technology, scientific research, investigations, and in daily life to trigger warnings about safety and to build familiarity. Like a tree trunk's rings record history in a pattern, disruption shows up in products and services—in an orderly recognizable pattern that consistently illuminate customers' expectations; they are markers of disruption. There are also choices that are framed around decision-making or maneuvers inside the pattern. The existence of this pattern could present a challenge for any company introducing a disruptive innovation without complete awareness. It could mean a company focused on the original theory's "simplicity, convenience, accessibility, and affordability" assumptions of disruptive innovation would miss future disruptions. It also means leaders would not develop the ambidextrous decision-making abilities required to interpret dynamic landscapes and avoid being disrupted.

The Innovator's Guide to Growth, a book affiliated with a consultancy practice cofounded by Christensen, suggested the need for a pattern on the last page of the book:

> Today's world presents vast opportunities for companies seeking to build competitive advantage through innovation. In any domain, people solve problems in a predictable way. When they first encounter a new type of challenge, they must solve it using an unstructured, trial-and-error approach. Over time, as understanding of the challenge grows, clear rules emerge to guide problem-solving efforts.
>
> We believe that the concept innovation is in transition between a theory of random trial and error and perfectly predictable paint-by-number rules. We think of this transitional period as the "era of pattern recognition." (Anthony et al. 2008)

The inspirations behind my *Pattern of Disruptions* for products, services, and business models resulted from a synthesis of a number of sources: key published works and observed phenomena of disruptive innovation that redefined customers' expectations and value creation from my years as an innovation practitioner and business leader. Then I tested the pattern with digital products, for example the mobile phone and the smart phone, as well as products transitioning to digital, for example the Swiffer® and Magna Seating's reconfigurable interiors. This and other examples are highlighted in this book. Each disrupter builds on the capabilities unlocked in the prior.

- Accessible—originated from Christensen's original theory of disruptive innovation in *The Innovator's Dilemma*.
- Dependable—originated from the global acceptance of quality standards and Downes' *Big Bang Disruption* theory of disruptive innovation.
- Reliable—originated from the advantages of digital to replicate, to store, to protect, and to secure assets.

> - Usable—originated from Steve Jobs at Apple. He combined innovations into devices, such as the iPhone, evolving the devices' intended digital purposes (calls, texts and emails), as well as developing features and platforms to enable the devices' ease-of-use.
> - Delightful—originated from Jeff Bezos at Amazon. He elevated the importance of delivering on customer experience.
> - Meaningfulness—originated from megatrends focused on planet-scale concerns.

There are major categories of escalating customers' expectations. They reveal a pattern that I call out in the *DICE Theory*. They are the *Pattern of Disruptions*, an innovation lifecycle of major categories of customers' expectations. The patten can be used to track changes in value creation, changes in purchasing behaviors, and changes with capabilities and technologies (Figure 1.2). The pattern is not a checklist. It is an innovation lifecycle.

- "Accessible": breaking down barriers to ownership and consumption;
- "Dependable": quality, measured by uptime;
- "Reliable": infrastructure safety (assets) and digital networks (data);
- "Usable": expanded utility for purposes not originally intended often enabled by digital connectivity;
- "Delightful": intense focus on user experience through a digital platform (or multisided platform); and
- "Meaningfulness": targets megatrends, for example: climate change and sustainability; urbanization; aging; disparities and inequalities.

Three disrupters (reliable, usable, and delightful) rely on the advancement and the proliferation of digital technologies throughout society. They require new infrastructure, new technologies, and new business rules (i.e. digital transformation). The last disrupter will require companies to develop new value networks, innovation and business ecosystems, and digitally network them.

Meaningfulness:
targets Megatrends,
e.g. climate change
and sustainability;
urbanization; aging;
disparities and
inequalities

Accessible:
breaks down
barriers to
ownership/
consumption

Delightful: intense
focus on user
experience through a
digital platform (or
multisided platform).

Pattern of
Disruptions
Categories of
Customers'
Expectations

Dependable:
quality,
measured by
uptime.

Usable: expanded utility
for purposes not
originally intended
enabled by digital
connectivity.

Reliable:
safety (asset)
and security
(data).

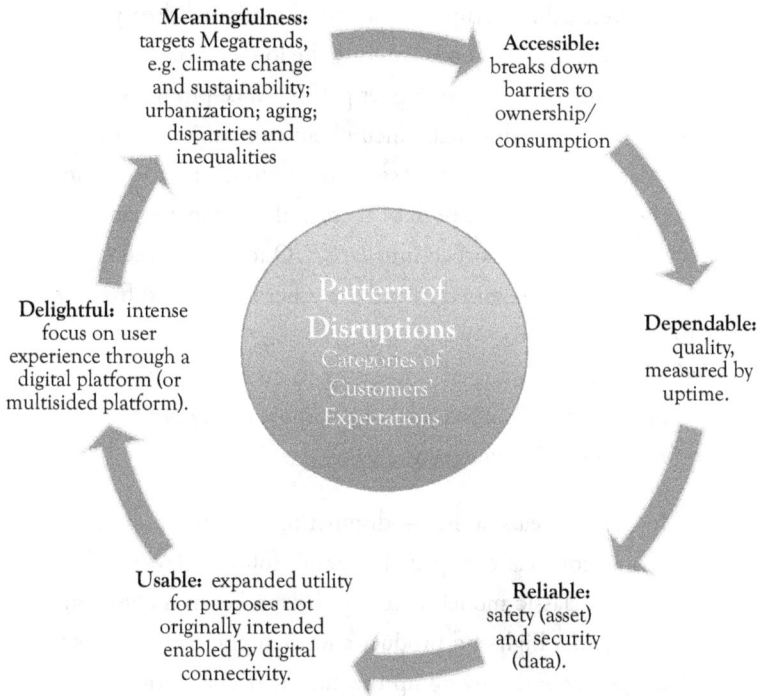

Figure 1.2 Major categories of customers' expectations: Pattern of Disruptions

I brought forward other theories to inform the *Pattern of Disruptions*:

- Digital is the tipping point. It has been changing the rules of business since the modern-day Internet was created. It will be the force that disrupts markets and erupts into mass diversifications in innovation, business models, competitor cooperation, cocreation, and a multitude of products and services, all of which are vague concepts at best from this vantage point. *DICE* is necessary for companies to comprehend the future of disruption. Digital transformation is a broad umbrella of initiatives that an organization takes in order to capture value and opportunities from integrating digital technologies into its products, processes, operations, and services (Furr et al. 2019).

- There were other disruptions besides the original theory's reliance on cheaper goods entering the low-end of the market and moving upmarket to higher performance products and services, thereby displacing incumbent companies' offerings. Two different authors proposed expansions or improvements to the original theory. Both of these authors' theories and observations are absorbed into *DICE*. One is conveyed exactly as the authors presented it, and the other is modified from its suggested version.
  - The exact meaning of "increasing in quality" to move upmarket is absorbed from the authors of *Big Bang Disruption* (Downes et al. 2015).

    In recent years a new—disquieting—form of disruptive innovation has emerged. It doesn't follow Clayton Christensen's classic model, entering the market as a cheap substitute to a high-end product and then gradually increasing in quality and moving up the customer chain. Instead, the innovation beats incumbents on both price and quality right from the start and quickly sweeps through every customer segment. This kind of "big bang" disruption can devastate entire product lines virtually overnight. Look at the effect that free navigation apps, preloaded on smartphones, had on the market for devices made by TomTom, Garmin, and Magellan. Big-bang disruptions often come out of the blue from people who aren't your traditional competitors. (Downes et al. 2015)
  - Downes modeled the observation and referred to disruptive innovations fitting this description as "big-bang disrupters" in the shape of a "Shark Fin." These disrupters did not fit into the original "dilemma" described by Christensen. These disrupters come out of "a function of near-perfect market information" (Downes et al. 2015). A poor reputation for quality in the digital age can ruin any brand and cost a company untold sums. This phenomenon is the result of disrupters enhancing quality and uptime demands on

products and services. (I illustrate the "Shark-Fin" shape and where it fits into *DICE* model in Chapter 2, Figure 2.1.)

o The other author whose theory is absorbed into *DICE* is Rogers' theory of disruption, as a two-sided approach across consumer purchase behaviors and business models. *DICE* defines consumer purchase behaviors, as customers' expectations, and not only on the basis of price or access, but as a pattern of major categories of customers' expectations for value creation throughout the innovation lifecycle. Also, *DICE* focuses on value through interactions of products, services, and business models. These interactions occur through networks that exceed the value that any one contributor brings to the marketplace. Like Rogers' theory, *DICE* unlocks value through interactions of "people, partners, assets and processes" (Rogers 2016). *DICE* has the added element of digital capabilities in business model platforms through digital transformation of products and services.

The origins for the decision patterns for the S curve innovation maneuvers later discussed used Rogers' theory as a catalyst, as well as key published works and observed phenomena of disruptions through digital business model innovation. I use Netflix as an example to illustrate how maneuvers through digital business models can disrupt. Furthermore, I highlight an example of the two dimensions of *DICE Theory* and their interactions (the *Pattern of Disruptions* for products/services and business models) using passenger vehicles and digital platform business models. Both examples are highlighted in this book.

Regarding the S curve of innovation, there are six maneuvers relevant for the dimensions in the *DICE Theory*:

- A company could expand within a disrupter, leaving very little market share available for competitors. [*Landside*: "the disrupter quickly takes over the entire market, pushing the incumbent into obscurity" (Rogers 2016)].

- A company can climb a curve to the top and then jump into the next curve.
- A company could recognize an upcoming shift in customers' expectations, climb with the market expansion before realizing its capabilities are unmatched for the climb. The company jumps to the next curve.
- A company could jump early in preparation for building its talent to climb the next curve, realizing the market is saturated. [*Splitting the market*: "with the disrupter's and the incumbent's business models each taking large shares" (Rogers 2016)].
- A company might jump and 'pause' before climbing—realizing it needs additional capabilities through partnerships.
- A company participates in a segment of the market. [*Niche* "where the disrupter is attractive to only a very specific portion of the market" (Rogers 2016)].

Later in the book I model the *DICE Theory* with its dimensions of value creation and the S curve of innovation. You will see how they feature in leaders' strategic choices and decision-making for disruptive innovation.

This book offers the breadcrumbs to follow through repeating patterns of disruptions and maneuverers that are revealed only in this book:

- It demonstrates that a pattern of disrupters exists to track major categories of customers' expectations for disruptive innovation. It highlights how over time these disrupters influence the success of products and the unfortunate demise of competitors that failed to recognize them.
- It absorbs past theories of disruptive innovation, as well as brings into focus three digital disrupters—never before addressed.
- It detects disruptions across all customer types for companies to position capabilities, resources, talent, and supply chain partners—to be the disrupter and not the disrupted. This predictive ability is what truly set it apart from other theories.

- It enables both incumbents and new entrants, as well as acts as an alarm to alert them to when they are being (or at risk of being) disrupted. For incumbents, it offers ambidextrous flexibility, leveraging innovation through core (incremental), adjacent (breakthrough), and transformational (disruptive) capabilities. For entrants, it informs them about needed innovation capabilities to maximize impact and lower uncertainties.
- It develops a new theory of disruptive innovation and models it to help companies manage multiple innovation S curve maneuvers.
- It is the only book—to my knowledge—that addresses the need to combine the capabilities of digital transformation with disruptive innovation to accelerate new growth across products, services, and business models for the 21st-century.

When Is "DICE Theory" Observable?

Here are the delimiters for the *Pattern of Disruptions*:

- The *Pattern of Disruptions* is immutable. After customers gain access to a disruptive innovation (product, service, or business model), they move on to create expectations for value creation and behaviors in the next disrupters. This triggers the next disrupters and redefines the focus of customers' future expectations.
- A product, service, or business model can be disrupted multiple times, including within the same disrupter. There can be multiple disruptions occurring until new customers' expectations are redefined to change purchasing behaviors— displacing the incumbent.
- Once a disruptive innovation redefines customers' expectations within a disrupter, the disruptive innovation starts the pattern over from the beginning, taking on its own path through the pattern, and leaving behind the product(s), service(s), or business model(s) it disrupted.

- A disruptive innovation that makes it to the last disrupter "meaningfulness" starts the pattern over from "accessible," taking with it all of the insights it acquired through the previous iterations.
- Disrupters are impacted by developments in previous disrupters. For instance, a new technology can enable a disrupter to expand its range of capabilities, creating a "ripple effect," for example, 5G in "reliable" will impact computing speeds that enable the next disrupters. ("Reliable" is undergoing such robust cycles of digital innovations that envisioning the impacts to the next disrupters appears to be cosmic predictions (way past conceivable). However, one of the purposes of *DICE* is directional guidance.)

Here is guidance for the S curve of innovation:

- Unlike the *Pattern of Disruptions*—defined by customers' expectations, the S curve maneuvers of a company to disrupt is determined by the company's talent, competition, and capability.
- Understanding these maneuvers within the S curve of innovation can extend the market for a product/service/business model innovation. They can guide companies to use technology to enable a product or service to meet customers' expectations. They can shift value created from a single-use product or service to a networked use product or service (business model digital platform).

Why Companies Can No Longer Put Off Developing Digital Transformation Plus Disruptive Innovation Capabilities?

The first versions of the Internet evolved into networks of networks, adding architectural infrastructure (or "backbones"), commercial providers (Internet Service Providers), and billions of connected "things." This combined with digital transformation is accelerating the speed of disruptive innovation. This should be of greatest concern to the majority of global companies in developed countries, as they have the most to lose in economic value from digital disruptions. Their markets are larger and scaled over decades. Their brands make their products and services recognizable across the globe. The historical knowledge of these incumbents is well documented in business cases, books, and online resources. They are invested in their current operating models—perfected through skilled labor force, supply chain partners, and industry standards. It will be difficult for these companies to adapt to a different set of rules, new operating models, and capabilities to create value.

Developed countries will defend these companies with nationalists political viewpoints. They will attempt to protect physical products at their geographic borders. This will momentarily stall digital disruptions to physical products. For now, digital disruptions do not recognize borders, which are creating another political frontier for developed countries— the Internet. There are ongoing battles over which Internet is allowed to operate and to have access to customers within a country's borders. "Sometimes virtual borders need to be erected, so that data do not leave or enter a certain country" (*The Economist* 2020). This includes data privacy regulations. "Data were supposed to float freely around the world to where they are most efficiently crunched. But flows are increasingly blocked by governments which seek to protect their country's people, sovereignty and economy" (*The Economist* 2020). This is causing what the technology industry calls "Splinternet," "a maze of national or regional and often conflicting rules" (*The Economist* 2020).

Nevertheless, once a "digital twin," a digital copy of a physical asset, is created then there is the potential for that asset to exist in "mirrored-economies," where a product is both physical and virtualized. The decoupling of products from their physical locations into digital twins eliminates a long-standing barrier to entry for entrants. Virtual products do not require the capital investments needed for physical products. This opens up opportunities for servicing both physical and virtual products. The COVID-19 global pandemic will stall digital disruptive innovations in physical products, but not for long. Time will pass, and while countries, cloud technology companies, and businesses fight over policies, legislation, and infrastructure, companies should prepare their senior leadership and midlevel managers to monitor developments closely to upgrade their digital capabilities. This book steers clear of policymaking and legislation, as these environments are fluid and any assumptions are inherently wrong from the start.

However, there is a more imminent threat posed by digital, and that is: products/services that are not digitally transformed—integrated with technology. They risk losing value to platform business models that unlock network effects. This book is a good first step for managers to prepare. It will help them explain what they are seeing in the marketplace. It will accelerate their intentional efforts to target ideas, opportunities, projects, and proposals for disruption. It will inform the decisions they make about resources to build the best capabilities for the challenges ahead. It will give them evidence from past disruptions, as well as help them explain what it means to be disrupted.

How Can Practitioners Apply DICE?

To demonstrate some of the ways the *DICE Theory* reaches different outcomes than the original theory of disruptive innovation—specifically for products and services, let us examine the smartphone market. The smartphone is a point of contention with the original theory of disruptive innovation. In fact, Christensen dismissed the iPhone as a disruptive innovation (Rogers 2016). The mobile cellphone market was established. Christensen did not acknowledge that there could be a digital disruption occurring in an established market for an existing product. He later attributed the smartphone disruption to the laptop market and not the cellphone market (Roger 2016). Therefore, all smartphone innovations following the laptop were considered performance improvements (incremental innovations) for a sustaining business.

This is how disruption plays out in the smartphone market using *DICE*. Motorola was the first to mass-produce a handheld mobile cellphone on April 3, 1973. The first smartphone followed 19 years later, in 1992. "It was called the Simon Personal Communicator, and it was created by IBM more than 15 [fifteen] years before Apple released the iPhone" (Tweedie 2015). The first version of the iPhone was released on June 29, 2007. It was Steve Jobs who recognized the need to disrupt the smartphone market at the "usable" disrupter; he carried it through to "delightful," and on to building a company valued at more than 300 billion dollars. Since Job's death Apple is worth more than three times that valuation. There is more to come from innovations in the "delightful" disrupter for smartphones—consider camera technologies for virtual reality and augmented reality—as well as in "meaningfulness" disrupter, with battery technologies and wireless charging technologies threatening to eliminate cables for charging (Table 1.1).

Table 1.1 Pattern of Disruptions and smartphone market

Major Categories of Customers' Expectations	Customer Needs	Disruptive Innovation Examples
Accessible	Expensive; limited to business professionals	Lower cost devices and plans
Dependable	Battery life, fires	External batteries, recalls, design phones to use less power
Reliable	Networks = certain geographies and cell towers	Expanded coverage areas and 3G, 4G, 5G
Usable	Unique accessories, data storage, music, apps	Interoperability devices/accessories, cloud storage, sharing platforms
Delightful	Fragmented community sharing, awkward pairing and configuring "connected" smart devices, for example, car, home, apps, etc.	User experience, multisided platform network effects, voice-interactive assistants
Meaningfulness	Materials impacting climate change, mining for cobalt, lithium, and recycling batteries	Virtualized product, dematerialized product design; European Union resolution to control e-waste, potentially requiring a common charger for smartphones—possibly wireless charging

Reflecting back on Gartners' *Hype Cycle* for emerging technologies, the original theory of disruptive innovation does not explain the phenomenon of what happens next, why innovations descend into the "Trough of Disillusionment" after entering the market? Or how can a company that invests in disruptive innovation at "accessible" hold on to and defend its investment? Is there an engine that could suspend the time the "Peak of Inflated Expectations" curve meets expectations? These questions are more relevant today, as we look to the Digital Transformation in the New Industrial Revolution (Industry 4.0) and the seismic shifts in technology. Digital will unlock disruptive innovations for many products/services/business models that are still awaiting the opportunity to enter the digital disrupters in the *Pattern of Disruptions*. In order to take advantage of digital disruptions, the processes within a company must be digitized to allow future leaders to access archives of innovations to determine future impacts, as well as to build data models for predictive analytics. This is an exciting time because it means innovations that never reached the digital disrupters in the *Pattern of Disruptions* are in play.

Digital is the innovation tipping point that shifts the competitive landscape, making it difficult to catch up. The digitally disruptive impacts occurring in the "reliable", "usable," "delightful," and "meaningfulness" disrupters will be faster and far more difficult to challenge due to platforms and networked ecosystems. The potential for network effects in digital takes over. This increases the advantages to the frontrunners, leaving very little market share available to competitors. It will not be the first time that a revolution offers opportunities for disruptive innovations.

How Is the Pattern of Disruptions Different than Another Set of Patterns?

Deloitte University Press (2015) conducted a comprehensive business case analysis on disruption, "looking for the specific ways threats manifest in a world." They uncovered nine *patterns of disruption*. Here are the delimiters *Deloitte* sets:

> These patterns are more than "one-off" occurrences, but they also are not universal forces; they are disruptions that will likely occur in more than one market but not in all markets; each delivers new value through a new approach subject to a set of market conditions; each brings its own challenges for the incumbent. (*Deloitte University Press 2015*)

Without the benefits of discussions with *Deloitte* and only the white paper it published on its website, I attempted to align its patterns in Table 1.2.

Table 1.2 Comparing the Pattern of Disruptions to other patterns

Pattern of Disruptions: Major Categories of Customers' Expectations	[Nine] Patterns of Disruptions (Deloitte University Press)
"Accessible": breaking down barriers to ownership/consumption	• Align price with use: reducing upfront barriers to use • Unbundle products and services: giving you just what you want, nothing more
"Dependable": quality, measured by uptime	
"Reliable": infrastructure safety (assets) and digital networks (data)	• Unlock adjacent assets: cultivating opportunities on the edge
"Usable": expanded utility for purposes not originally intended, often enabled by digital connectivity	• Expand marketplace reach: connecting fragmented buyers and sellers—whenever, wherever • Connect peers: fostering direct, peer-to-peer connections
"Delightful": intense focus on user experience through a digital platform (or multisided platform)	• Turn products into platforms: providing a foundation for others to build upon
"Meaningfulness": targets megatrends, for example, climate change and sustainability; urbanization; aging; disparities and inequalities	• Shorten the value chain: transforming fewer inputs into greater value outputs • Converge products: making 1+1 >2
	• Distribute product development: mobilizing many to create one

Observable distinctions between *Pattern of Disruptions* and Deloitte's patterns are as follows:

- *Pattern of Disruptions* offers a repeatable innovation lifecycle for products, services, and business models.
- It is robust and comprehensive—capturing the evolutionary lifecycle of innovations.
- It is not limited to certain industries, markets, or sectors.

Key Takeaways From Chapter 1

- Christensen's original theory was a first step in alerting incumbents to changing market conditions that threatened their leadership in existing B2B markets.

- Christensen missed a key warning to incumbents: the source of the threats to market leadership is changing consumer behaviors (based on major categories of customers' expectations for value creation, *Pattern of Disruptions*) that include digitally enabled products, services, and business models.
- Digital transformation is a set of capabilities that businesses must develop, which integrates digital to increase value to customers.
- *Pattern of Disruptions* is a guide for innovators and strategists to develop disruptive innovations.
- In addition to the value generation guidance in the pattern, business leaders can leverage maneuvers in the innovation S curve.
- The ability to disrupt across all dimensions in the *DICE Theory* requires ambidextrous leadership.
- *Part 1: It's the Background* is complete.

PART II

It's the Framework

CHAPTER 2

Modeling Theories of Disruptive Innovation

There are decades of published works on disruptive innovation. We covered the theories and how each evolved the original theory. Now we must reconcile the various models of disruptive innovation. There are several popular models of disruptive innovation published by leading business management schools: "Four Elements of the Theory of Disruptive Innovation" (King et al. 2015) published in an article in *MIT Sloan Management Review*, and "The Disruptive Innovation Model" published in *The Innovator's Solution* (Christensen et al. 2003) by *Harvard Business Review Press* (later updated in a *Harvard Business Review* article, "What is Disruptive Innovation?" (Christensen et al. 2015). There is another set of guidelines offered by *Deloitte University Press* that offers some interesting guidance, but they are not articulated in a model similar to the others. I will compare the *DICE Theory's* model to the other models as well as the guidelines by *Deloitte*. There are key similarities between the three models and the *DICE Model*. The most synergies exist with the "Four Elements of the Theory of Disruptive Innovation." However, there are contrasting differences. They are listed in the following Table 2.1.

Table 2.1 Key similarities between other disruptive innovation models and DICE

Disruptive innovation models	Key similarities aligned with DICE
Four Elements of the Theory of Disruptive Innovation (King and Baartartogtokh 2015)	• Descriptive approach: defensive and offensive competitive strategy • Incumbents can switch roles between disrupter and disrupted over time • A pathway for sustaining innovation within disruptive innovation • Disruptive innovations move upmarket
The Disruptive Innovation Model (Christensen, Raynor, and McDonald 2015)	• Descriptive approach: defensive and offensive competitive strategy • A pathway for sustaining innovation within disruptive innovation • Disruptive innovations move upmarket
The Disruptive Innovation Model (Christensen and Raynor 2003)	• Descriptive approach: defensive competitive strategy • A pathway for sustaining innovation within disruptive innovation • Disruptive innovations move upmarket

The Models

The "Four Elements of the Theory of Disruptive Innovation" (King et al. 2015) is a descriptive approach intended for both defensive and offensive competitive strategy to guide incumbent companies through scenarios, describing entry points for incumbents based on sustaining (incremental innovations) and transformational (disruptive innovations): (1) incremental innovations by incumbents that increase in performance; (2) incremental innovations by incumbents with performance improvements that exceed customers' needs "overshooting"; (3) disruptive innovations at the low-end performance markets below customers' needs; (4) incremental innovations by incumbents with performance attributes that are on a trajectory drastically different than customers' needs.

In comparison, *DICE* offers three approaches: descriptive, prescriptive, and predictive—each capable of being used for defensive and offensive strategy.

- It is descriptive; highlighting advantages for incumbents and new entrants, where one is favored over the other (based on access to customers).
- It is prescriptively comprehensive across all theories, starting with the original theory's premise of "accessible." It brings in the observations for "quality" by Downes (2013) marked by his Shark-Fin shape in Figure 2.1, which is captured in the "dependable" disrupter. It includes network infrastructure, data storage, and asset security reflected in the "reliable" disrupter. It introduces new disrupters "usable", "delightful" and "meaningfulness"—which are the results of my investigations scanning the edges of markets. These disrupters were not previously observed in the original theory or subsequent theories.
  - This pattern lays the foundation for the model. Within each disrupter there are forces, such as talent, competition, and capabilities, that impact how companies maneuver and how they innovate. Until customers' expectations have been redefined and consumers' purchasing behaviors changed (i.e. disrupted), companies continue maneuvering and innovating. It can take decades or centuries for a product, service, or business model to be disrupted, but when it happens it unlocks other disrupters in the pattern. The current disruptive innovation becomes the starting point for innovations in the next disrupter. Each time a company enters a new disrupter it must recalibrate against these forces and capabilities.
- It is predictive, timing disruptions in accordance with the *Pattern of Disruptions*. This timing and alignment are how companies avoid "overshooting" and escape the fall into the *Hype Cycle's* "Trough of Disillusionment."

The model in Figure 2.1 illustrates the descriptive, prescriptive, and predictive aspects of the *DICE Theory*.

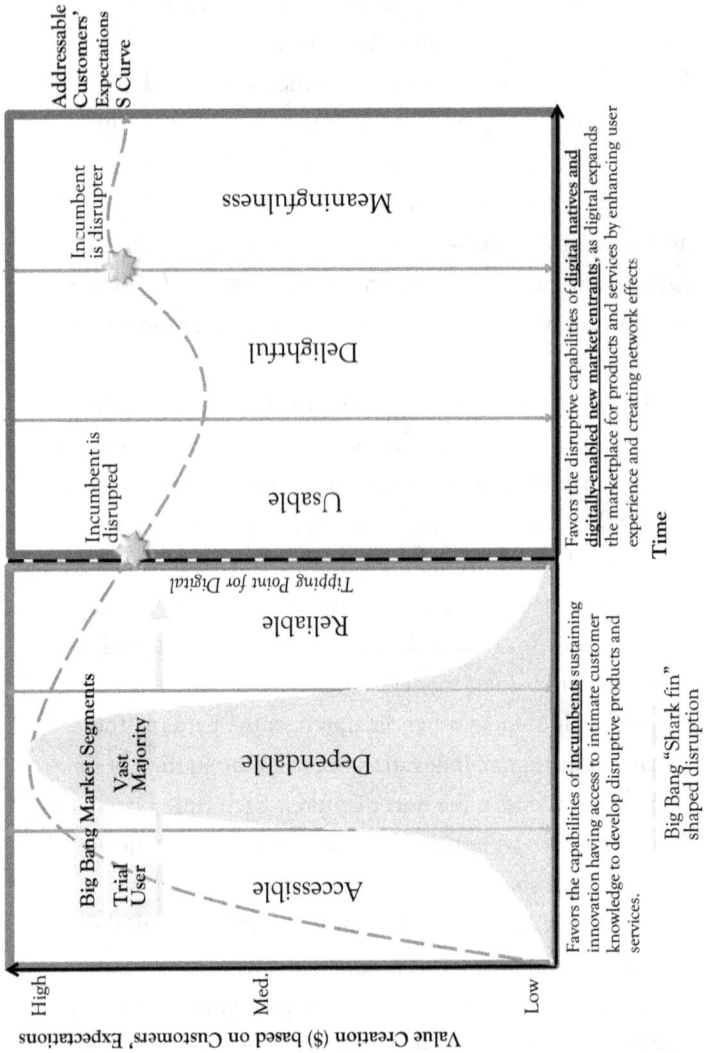

Figure 2.1 Disruptive Innovation Customers' Expectations model

There are three (3) dimensions in *DICE*:

- Saturation level (1), which defines the limits of customers' expectations that could result in value creation over time. It is marked in the figures as an innovation S curve "Addressable Customers' Expectations S Curve."
- *Pattern of Disruptions* house the other two dimensions, which determines how value is created, captured, and delivered. The disrupters are labeled in Figure 2.1:
  - Products/services (2).
  - Business models (3), (including digital platform business models).

The MIT Team and Christensen models have a directional straight line indicating the path of disruption for entrants and incumbents. *DICE* challenges the straight-line assumption. A key differentiator of the model for the *DICE Theory* centers on the "Addressable Customers' Expectations S Curve" in Figure 2.1. It describes the critical value creation relationship between customers' expectations (not performance) and consumers' purchasing behaviors. "In a longitudinal, multiple-case study, McDermott and O'Conner (2002) observed that too much effort was put into the technical development of new products rather than the analysis of potential markets and the refinement of business plans" (Reinhardt et al. 2011). Customers' expectations inherently capture performance within their willingness to pay. The overall height of the innovation S curve represents the maximum value creation that an innovation can generate while meeting customers' expectations, which also represents the saturation levels. This is important because customers will react inconsistently to disruptive innovations as they move upmarket. Therefore, the curve will ebb and flow.

Whereas other models are descriptive, the prescriptive and predictive abilities of *DICE* are what truly set it apart from the other models. They are the most powerful aspects of this model. They inform strategic choices, enable insights, and trigger alarms for both incumbents and new entrants. They offer companies foresight, a few disruptions ahead of competitors, to position capabilities, resources, and supply chain partners—to be the disrupter and not the disrupted. The combinations of all the key elements in the *DICE* model describe a dynamic environment that helps companies to navigate disruptive innovation and digital transformation.

There are three (3) alerts in the model shown in Figure 2.1 marked with "star" icons and a vertical dashed line labeled "Tipping Point for Digital":

1. The first "star" alerts incumbents to a critical tipping point for digital capabilities in the "reliable", "usable", and "delightful" disrupters. The higher costs to digitally integrate products could reduce the size of the market and the potential for higher profits. The smaller market size could cause incumbents to abandon these markets, leaving them undefended, which opens up opportunities for entrants. Traditionally access to customers held back new entrants from sustaining innovations. With digital the speed of customer acquisition can be overcome, eliminating this incumbent advantage.

2. The second "star" alerts entrants to the "meaningfulness" disrupter, which offers opportunities for the incumbent to be the disrupter. This disrupter in the pattern can be challenging for an entrant. It requires vast resources and a supply chain to leverage. A mature supply chain and partners enhance maneuverability, both of which are capabilities inherently benefiting incumbents.

3. The dashed line "*Tipping Point for Digital*" indicates a shift in the value formula digital creates over time. The value formula is the sum value of products + services + business models (÷) divided by costs. The weight in the value created by products and services (disruptive innovations in "accessible" and "dependable") is almost displaced by business models (disruptive innovations in "reliable", "usable", "delightful", and "meaningfulness"). This shift severely disadvantages companies without digital capabilities.

There are fewer similarities between the *DICE* model and the two versions of *The Disruptive Innovation Model* (2003-version and 2015-version). However, it is worthwhile to note the evolution between the two versions. There are two minor distinctions between the two versions.

The first minor distinction is the range for profitability in the 2015-version "Performance That Customers Can Utilize or Absorb" replaced the earlier 2003-version's "Range of Performance That Customers Can Utilize." This can be explained, as a reinterpretation of the impacts of performance ranges on price points. Overall, the message remains the same: customers purchase products based on performance. When a sustaining innovation progresses along a technology trajectory that increases the price without matching customers' needs to the product's utilization customers cannot absorb the performance improvements over time, resulting in "overshooting." In the worst cases, companies deploying resources to capture upmarket profits leaves low-end markets undefended. Christensen and Raynor (2003) called this "asymmetric motivation", and the essence of the innovator's dilemma. New entrants can enter the market at a lower price point, focusing on the critical performance factors that align with the majority of customers' needs and advance upmarket with new products. The second minor distinction was adding trajectories on parallel paths to the 2015-version: one for "sustaining" with incumbents and the other for "disruptive" entrants. This characterizes the movements and behaviors of incumbents versus entrants. The idea that the path for the incumbent and the path for the entrant is different and that they would not crossover is consistent with Christensen's books on the original theory. This is a departure from both "Four Elements" and *DICE*, which recognizes that innovation capabilities play a role in a company's abilities to react to disruptions, and there are maneuvers available to them, as innovators, that are not based on being an incumbent or an entrant.

There is a similarity between the two versions of *The Disruptive Innovation Model* and the "Four Elements of the Theory of Disruptive Innovation." They both use "performance" as determinants for disruptive innovation. This is where they depart from *DICE*, which focuses on customer expectations for value creation, as determinants in consumers purchasing behaviors. Enhancing performance is only valuable to customers when they can both accept and absorb the improved performances. Disruptions built on performance criteria without the perspective of market pull from customers' expectations results in "overshooting." Performance is absolutely a factor in disruptive innovation. However, it is not the determining factor.

Deloitte University Press (2015) defined some maneuvers that are interesting. They could be implied outcomes for both the "Four Elements of the Theory of Disruptive Innovation" and *DICE* models. Unmet customers' needs invite fragmented players to satisfy tiers of customers within the larger market; entrants siphon off market share from incumbents, but not completely displacing them; customers' needs migrate away from the incumbent toward a new approach that moves the entire market; and market consolidations through incumbent mergers and acquisitions.

Despite the existence of the disruptive innovation models to guide leaders' decisions, there are unexpected events that complicate any model:

- Disruptive innovations can end prematurely (derailed, stalled, or stopped)—for instance, based on influencers in social networks or customer reviews.
- Complacency is another killer of disruption that can never be overemphasized.
- A company could misjudge the timing of the market and "leapfrog" too early to disrupt, leaving behind opportunities for disruption for another company that wholly understands customers' expectations.
- A company could scare away consumers due to questionable business practices or concerns about product liability and ethics.
- The application or industry could be heavily regulated, creating barriers to entry for disruptive innovations.
- Companies can lose sight of disruptions outside of its market vantage, that is, it supplies into a system, or it is a service provider that is limited by a manufacturer's designs, processes, or other policies.
- Then there is the potential for shifts in technology.

More Than Meets The Eye

As a reminder, the *DICE Theory* has three dimensions; two of the dimensions are products/services and business models. The products/services anchor the business models. The dynamics between them must be clearly understood. A rule of thumb for disruptive innovation: *A product/service must be stable (i.e. customers' expectations have been redefined and consumers' behaviors have changed) before the product/service can be used in a business model to disrupt.* A product/service in flux is an unstable foundation to build a business model. The interactions between the two dimensions (product/service and business model) create the value formula.

I demonstrate why this rule is important using the current internal combustion engine (ICE) passenger vehicle automotive market. It is one of the oldest markets in the world. Assuming the history of the automobile is well documented then it is not presumptuous that its disruptive innovations can be easily tracked through the *Pattern of Disruptions:* "accessible', "dependable" and "reliable", and interpreted through the lenses of the *DICE Theory.* Therefore, in the interests of time, let us pick up the pattern for the passenger vehicle (product) with the most recent digital disrupters: "usable", "delightful", and "meaningfulness." We find that all 3 disrupters are simultaneously happening in the passenger vehicle market:

1. The product is in the "usable" disrupter: fully autonomous advanced driver-assistance systems (ADAS), as well as developing technology enablers: cloud connectivity, cameras, sensors, and software.
2. There are disruptive innovations in the "delightful" disrupter focused on the connected traveller across mobility applications and modes of transportation. There were already estimates of the value digital could create. "Our analysis suggests that there is a $0.7 trillion opportunity to create value from the digital transformation of the automotive industry, through initiatives such as channel migration to virtual purchases, value-added subscriptions and next generation servicing" (a report by *World Economic Forum* and *Accenture,* 2019).
3. Disruptive innovations in "meaningfulness" to dematerialize automotive passenger car interiors were on display at *Consumer Electronics Show* (CES) 2020 industry events in Las Vegas, Nevada. Tier One Suppliers of automotive interiors showcased "speakerless" audio systems (Continental Sennheiser), voice assistants that promised over-the-air (OTA) software updates that rapidly refreshed features, and virtualized products that replaced hardware (knobs, switches, and

buttons), including one that replaced the physical visor with transparent panels that darken based on the driver's eyes and the position of the sun (Bosch).

To add onto the ongoing digital disruptions occurring in the ICE passenger vehicle market (product), it is also being disrupted with digital business model innovations. In 1913, Henry Ford started the original single household user business model for passenger cars when he installed the first moving assembly lines to mass-produce an entire automobile. Around 2012 technology companies in the Bay-area of California digitally integrated the vehicle with telematics, apps, and a digital platform to transform the vehicle from a single household user business model to a peer-to-peer user business model. Profitability has been a consistent challenge for peer-to-peer mobility business models. Ride hailing, ridesharing, and mobility fleets (Mobility-On-Demand and Mobility-As-A-Service) have not reached the expected revenue potential, partly due to low utilization. A digital platform business model cannot generate profits without mass customer and partner engagement that generates network effects. For instance, in 2018 Daimler and BMW announced a merger of the manufacturers' car-sharing services with an investment of one billion Euros. One year later, the merged car sharing service is considered a "flop." Admittedly profitability was blamed along with the changes in CEOs at both companies (*Fockenbrock* 2019). Although the lack of profits were to blame, the *DICE Theory* and model points toward another suspect: customers' expectations at "usable" for the passenger vehicle (product) have not been redefined, resulting in changing consumers' behaviors. Customers' expectations for the passenger vehicle at the "usable" disrupter are unsettled.

Also, the *DICE Theory* predicts that the other disruptions already underway ("delightful" and "meaningfulness") lack the footing of redefined customers' expectations from "usable" to make them successful at being disruptive. Each disrupter in the pattern builds upon the redefined customers' expectations and the capabilities unlocked in the prior disrupters. It is a worthwhile debate to consider what vehicle will emerge out of the "usable" disrupter. The disruptive innovations for the next disrupters hinge upon these outcomes. How will the new version of the incumbent

ICE, disrupted in "usable", redefine customers' expectations, changing consumers' behaviors, and what new path will it take onto "delightful"? It is yet to be determined. COVID-19 will inevitably create innovations in the "usable" disrupter. Stay tuned.

Automotive—like many other established markets—face a challenge to manage both dimensions through the *Pattern of Disruptions*. This example demonstrates the difficulties for incumbents with established products, defending against disruptions while maintaining a focus on the core business' operating model. Notwithstanding, these are the new rules of business in the 21st-century. It is no longer a safe position to consider one dimension of innovation. Failing to manage these complexities threatens a company's abilities to remain relevant with customers and to capture customers' insights to continue tracking possible disruptions through changes in customers' expectations that lead to changes in consumer purchasing behaviors. Managing multiple disruptions in this dynamic environment is the new normal. It is a complicated balancing act, and it is not isolated to incumbents. It presents a unique challenge for any company with an established product. The incumbent ICE vehicle is proof that even one hundred years of insights cannot buffer incumbent companies from disruptive innovations. No company is safe from disruption.

> The model predicts that after "dependable", products/services will be more stable, which makes them a target for third party business model innovators. The way to defend the value created by products/services is to integrate them with technology (i.e. digital transformation) and to develop business models to unlock additional value through networks. Without this digital transformation products/services/business models are at risk of losing their value to a third party company's digital business model. This is the "Tipping Point" in Figure 3.1.

Conflicts and Doubts

One could argue that sharing the *DICE Theory* and model makes disruptive innovation accessible, thereby increasing everyone's capacity to grow, ultimately leading to more innovations and competition. This is true. However, it takes more than knowing the elements in *DICE* to be successful at execution. This is why I go beyond my theory into actionable guidance and relevant use cases to help companies to better understand disruptive innovation and its complementary capabilities through digital transformation. Product innovations with the potential to follow the pattern must first exist and creating them from the start will require enormous investments. Resources, processes, and operations cannot be replaced by a pattern. Leaders should not make the mistake of diminishing internal capabilities in favor of a pattern or an algorithm—disruptive innovation strategy needs to exist within context. This is why I offer guidance to companies on developing innovation maturity, where its capabilities are strongest and where there are gaps. (More on this in *Chapter Six: Hold the Line and Prepare to Advance*).

One could argue, if every company follows the same pathway to disruptive innovations then no company's strategy is safe from being picked off by competitors. Concealing insights does not protect a company's strategy from being replicated. This is already happening whether or not leaders acknowledge it. There is tons of searchable information available on the Internet, as well as third-party companies selling content. A company can purchase another's products to perform competitive benchmark analysis. None of this changes whether companies open their physical or virtual doors everyday to compete. In this way, now management can accelerate their innovation portfolios with markers consistent with the patterns, develop new business models, evaluate new growth opportunities, and reevaluate shelved or discarded projects.

Excellent places to start investigating the potential for disruptive innovations are within the company's products, shelved ideas, and projects, as well as archived research and experiments, prototypes, testing, and data. Some version of this statement has been made about leadership and management in the U.S. Navy: "There are no new ideas in the Navy." Well, there are very few new ideas in civilian life, which means most ideas have gone through the *Pattern of Disruptions* at least once. Many established markets have millions of products and services that have gone through the pattern at least once, which means there are lessons-learned and 'brilliant failures' that can be leveraged to accelerate future disruptions. I demonstrate how to locate the last disrupter to pick up the pattern for a disruptive innovation in the next chapter. Companies should generate target lists that teams can use to begin the process of mapping the *Pattern of Disruptions* for those products, ideas, and projects to identify areas of opportunity for disruption. Remember the earlier discussions on business model innovators building off of stable products? This is another area to consider after you confirmed customers' expectations for the product are not shifting. I demonstrate how to do this with my customer experience paradigm in the next chapter in the section on *Driving Innovation Outcomes*.

Furthermore, I caution against companies viewing the availability of the *DICE Theory* in the literature as justification to erect barriers to the outside world. It cannot be understated that broadening the teams that identify areas of opportunity to include external partnerships will greatly increase the capabilities of those teams. (More on this in *Chapter Seven: Open Innovation and Networked Ecosystems*). An increase in the roles of external partners across business and innovation ecosystems can accelerate disruptive innovations, including increasing ways to network those ecosystems to support business models, bringing in opportunities from strategic customers, entrepreneurs, government labs, and suppliers. Bringing the outside in is a skill and developing that capability will benefit any company willing to manage the risks of partnering and collaborating. This is not an easy task for most companies. It is well documented that an organization's dysfunctional culture can impede innovation. According to a 2016 Gartner Financial Services Innovation Survey, "the biggest threat to innovation is internal politics and an organizational culture which doesn't accept failure, doesn't accept ideas from outside, and/or cannot change" (Cancialosi 2017). A theory will not magically alter a company's culture. More discussions are needed to help a company better understand its internal capabilities and where external partnerships offer advantages.

Key Takeaways From Chapter 2

- There are three popular models of disruptive innovation, as well as another set of guidelines for a different set of patterns of disruption. They use performance as determinants of value creation for disruptive innovation. *DICE* focuses on customers' expectations for value creation.

- The *DICE* model is robust and comprehensive: descriptive, prescriptive, and predictive.
- *DICE* is a complex model with three dimensions: two dimensions are captured in the *Pattern of Disruptions* (products/services and business models), and the third dimension an innovation S curve that governs saturation levels. These combined elements create interactions and choices for companies with deep understandings of disruptive innovation and digital capabilities. In the next chapter, I discuss the strategic choices.
- The combined elements in the *DICE* model create a dynamic environment for business leaders to navigate and to maneuver. It cautions against prioritizing business model innovations with products/services that are experiencing disruptive innovations, which are redefining customers' expectations, value creation, and purchasing behaviors.

CHAPTER 3

Challenging the Innovation Mindset

Other disruptive innovation books describe various scenarios of incumbents fleeing from entrants, who create solutions that are better aligned with customers' expectations; the incumbent ignores the entrant until it can no longer compete against the entrant's lower prices; the incumbent concedes the low-end; eventually the entrant moves upmarket threatening higher margins and chasing the incumbent out of its market leadership positions. This book offers incumbents an alternative scenario. Given the option of foresight, it is likely that most incumbents would be better prepared to defend against these types of threats. Moreover, they can plan ahead for them. This does not mean that a decision to concede the low-end of a market or an unprofitable business will never be the best decision for an incumbent. This book offers incumbents foresight to avoid making rash decisions when facing unsuspecting disruptions. The *Pattern of Disruptions* allows a company's innovation organization to scan and to process the environment. It helps companies interpret what they are seeing or sensing. However, companies must do the work to identify disruptive innovations in the *Pattern of Disruptions*.

In the context of this book "customer categories" refer to any buyer or end-user: business-to-consumer (B2C), business-to-business (B2B), business-to-distributor-to-consumer (B2D2C). The *Pattern of Disruptions* finds no reason to distinguish between the categories. For instance, *Table 3.1: Comparing Pattern of Disruptions to Other Disrupters* shows how four other disrupters, specific to B2B markets by Grove in *Selling Solutions Isn't Enough*, fit into the *DICE Theory*:

Table 3.1 Comparing Pattern of Disruptions to other disrupters

Pattern of Disruptions: major categories of customers' expectations	Dynamics of most B2B markets disrupted by four factors (Grove et al. 2018)
"Accessible": breaking down barriers to ownership/ consumption	The abundance of product information. Easy access to information means that B2B customers can do research on their own before the formal sales process begins. Therefore, customers are less inclined to ask, "What does your product do?" than "What can it do for *me*?"
	A shift from cost to value. Procurement at customer organizations used to focus almost solely on negotiating for the lowest price. Today, it's aimed at identifying the supplier that can help generate the greatest business value.
"Dependable": quality, measured by uptime;	The commoditization of quality. The technical and qualitative differences between competing offerings have been dramatically narrowed by the widespread adoption of total quality management, Six Sigma, and similar methodologies. As a result, high quality has become table stakes, and companies need to deliver additional forms of value.
"Reliable": infrastructure safety (assets) and digital networks (data);	
"Usable": expanded utility for purposes not originally intended often enabled by digital connectivity;	In many industries, new technologies such as cloud computing, mobile applications, and artificial intelligence pose an existential threat to some business models because they offer cheaper and simpler ways to deliver the same functionality.
"Delightful": intense focus on user experience through a digital platform (or multisided platform);	
"Meaningfulness": targets megatrends, e.g. climate change and sustainability; urbanization; aging; disparities and inequalities	

In the past, customer categories helped companies align their purchasing decisions and buying behaviors. These are not to be ignored. However, they do not give innovators insights into the "why?" The pattern helps innovators interpret customers' expectations. All customers have expectations for buying products and services. The significance of understanding innovations through these lenses is to focus them. I give examples of methods innovators can use to reveal those expectations.

Driving Innovation Outcomes

There are several outcome-driven innovation methodologies for digital marketers that I will highlight as part of an effective disruptive innovation and digital transformation strategy, using the *DICE Theory*. I separate them as follows to draw out some relevant benefits (in order: job mapping, process mapping, observations, and market segmentation). The *Pattern of Disruptions* has an especially positive impact on segmenting. It expands its potential to identify customers' expectations across a broad spectrum of consumers. So I spend more time highlighting this method. All of the methodologies can be used to complement one another. Side-by-side comparisons can reveal areas for improvement. Combined they can lead to improved insights. Innovators should layer them and use outcomes from several methods to reach their innovation goals.

Jobs mapping, process mapping, observing, and segmenting are not new approaches for digital marketers; however, *DICE*—particularly its *Pattern of Disruptions*—creates perspectives to enhance these methods and leads to unique innovation outcomes. The pattern identifies where a product, service, or business model was last disrupted to drive an intentional starting point for discovering customers' needs and customers' expectations ripe for innovations. This is where companies should begin the processes of jobs mapping, process mapping, and observing. Later, I illustrate how the pattern can be used to accelerate a company's outcome-driven innovation efforts by closing in on the place to disrupt next. The *Pattern of Disruptions* bring the power of foresight.

In addition to the pattern expanding upon these known approaches for outcome-driven innovation, the pattern suggests where outcome innovations fit into a company's innovation portfolio: incremental sustaining, breakthrough adjacent, and disruptive transformational. For instance: when there is evidence that a product, service, business model has not been disrupted (i.e. customer expectations have not been redefined and changed consumer purchasing behaviors) to unlock the next disrupter in the pattern then incremental or adjacency innovations are best suited—not disruption.

Also many outcomes—at first glance—might appear not to fit into a company's sustaining business, but on second examination they "fit quite well with the company's existing business model; are called *adjacencies*" (Johnson 2018). Companies should examine their work to drive outcomes across their portfolio. A company would be misguided if it did not maintain a focus on pursuing all types of innovations. Innovating should be a part of the business DNA. This is one way to increase the chances a company will not miss a disrupter in the *Pattern of Disruptions*. Later, I illustrate an example of what happened to a company that missed, ignored, or mismanaged disruptive innovations. I will use the pattern to shed light on the missteps.

Job mapping:

Bettencourt and Anthony Ulwick in their collaborative article, "Turn Customers Input into Innovation", defined job mapping: "breaks down the task the customer wants done into a series of discrete process steps" (Bettencourt et al. 2008). The definition was built off work done by Ulwick on outcome-based methodology (Bettencourt et al. 2008). In disruptive innovation, companies are seeking to redefine customers' expectations (current, latent, and future)—some of these customers will not have a clear articulation of their expectations, others will have no experiences to draw on, and yet others will have limited experiences, having used some version of other products, services, or business models. For companies seeking to disrupt, I recommend starting with jobs mapping (focused on: What is the intent or effort?).

> A company can create value in a number of ways—by improving the execution of specific job steps; eliminating the need for particular inputs or outputs; removing an entire step from the responsibility of the customer; addressing an overlooked step; resequencing the steps; or enabling steps to be completed in new locations or at different times. (Bettencourt et al. 2008)

Process mapping:

For companies with sustaining innovations, looking to be disruptive, I recommend starting with current state process mapping (focused on: What's actually happening?). Process mapping is ideal for incremental improvements favorable for sustaining innovations. The advantage is to identify the "untouchables" (e.g. contracts, regulations, and compliance standards) in a customer's current state processes. These are elements in their processes that cannot be easily altered, changed, or eliminated. The worst things you can do is complete the exhaustive work of process mapping to find out that the innovations you identified are unmovable or restricted. So reveal those in the early stage discussions, and then ask the customer to review the process map to ensure you have a complete understanding of the current state.

Observations:

The goal of disruptive innovation is to redefine customers' expectations that lead to changes in consumer purchasing behaviors. This requires looking at all consumers through a new lens. It is difficult and likely frustrating to be in a new market with very little information or customer insights to draw upon. However, this is the nonconsumption market that leads to accelerated growth. It is worth the efforts. "According to [Clayton M. Christensen, Mark W. Johnson and Darrell K. Rigby] research, the probability of creating a successful, new growth business is 10 times greater if the innovators pursue a disruptive strategy rather than a sustaining one" (2002).

To identify consumers for disruptive innovation products, you must observe them—start to finish—completing tasks with alternatives and substitute products or services—to understand what problems they are looking to solve—take notice of what happens before the tasks starts and what happens when the tasks ends (use job mapping to document your observations). The key is to get as close as possible to observe consumers, to develop problem statements and corresponding hypotheses, then ask consumers a series of *why-questions?* It is worthless to ask what they want from a product that does not exist. Consumers understand their point of view and the context for their expectations—not those of other consumers. "Peter Drucker made this observation nearly a half-century ago, when he said that customers are always more interested in their outcome than in your solution" (Grove 2018). Furthermore, they are not experts on your companies' capabilities, "asking customers for solutions tends to undermine the innovation process" (Ulwick 2014).

For example, look for opportunities to observe within the framework of the *Pattern of Disruptions* and to inquire about customers' expectations within the categories. It is important to be expansive when uncovering disruptive innovations that will redefine customers' expectations. Two examples of observing consumers in an existing market for disruptive innovations:

> Magna Seating: The company used rich digital and in-market consumer research in China, Europe, and the United States to understand the views of the consumer when it comes to their personal experiences with seats. After observing consumers in their daily lives, Magna created an innovative seating platform focused on delivering the ideal user experience. From carrying cargo and fostering conversation on a long car ride to enabling a mobile meeting space during a ride share, Magna is developing reconfigurable seating solutions and technologies to reshape the vehicle cabin (*Magna Corporation* 2018).
>
> Continuum Innovation (Proctor and Gamble, Swiffer®): Our team began by conducting ethnographic research with target customers—in other words, visiting their homes and watching them clean their floors. Upon entering people's houses, we noticed something right away: The floors were already clean! Although they knew the intent of our visit, people still felt compelled to tidy up in anticipation of our arrival. This signaled a fundamental insight into the home cleaning experience: it's value-laden. Our floors are a reflection of ourselves (*Continuum Innovation* 2020).

To illustrate how observing works using the *Pattern of Disruptions*, let's use Swiffer®. First, I would suggest the Swiffer® team of Continuum Innovation examine the history of the traditional mop and track the disruptive innovations through the pattern to determine where current customers' expectations have stabilized.

The mop is a patented invention that is part of social history as well as the evolution of house wares. Thomas W. Steward, an African-American inventor, was awarded Patent Number 499,402 on June 13, 1893, for inventing the mop. His creation joined a long list of household equipment invented by African-Americans. The roster includes the eggbeater, yarn holder, ironing board, and bread-kneading machine. Steward's deck mop, made of yarn, quickly became well used for household and industrial cleaning. A wringing mechanism made the process of mopping and cleaning the mop easier and faster.

Another pair of inventors, brothers Peter and Thomas Vosbikian, fled Europe just before World War I and patented over 100 inventions in 30 years. In 1950, Peter Vosbikian developed a sponge mop that used a lever and flat strip of metal to press against the wet mop and squeeze it dry. This automatic mop eliminated the need to bend over and wring the mop repeatedly by hand. Its development was aided by the many technological improvements in the plastics industry that grew out of World War II and made absorbent plastic mop heads possible.

Other modifications have made mops even more adaptable to different cleaning chores. In 1999, Scotch Brite released a new wet mop made of natural cellulose and reinforced with internal polyester net. The cellulose does not leave lint like a cloth mop and absorbs 17 times its dry weight (Madehow.com 2020).

I would have noticed that traditional mops surpassed "accessible": breaks down barriers to ownership/consumption, "dependable": quality, measured by uptime with sponge mop heads and later the cellulose material mop head, and "reliable": safety with a handle wringing and release mechanism. The last disruptive innovation in the pattern for the traditional mop was "usable": expanded utility for purposes not originally intended often enabled by digital connectivity. I would have started there, which is where the Swiffer® team found customers tiding up floors in time for Swiffer® team to visit, which included the arduous process of dragging out the mops, buckets, and cleaners. These customer observation visits led to the development of Swiffer®. However, the aspects of digital connectivity in "usable" were missed or ignored by the Swiffer® Team.

There was more to come for this product, think digital connectivity and automation, iRobot® Braava jet® m6 (6110) Wi-Fi® Connected Robot Mop. The traditional mop is now being disrupted at "delightful": intense focus on user experience through a digital platform (or multisided platform) with the addition of digital platforms Alexa® or Google Voice Assistant. So a disruptive innovation developed over 123-years after the traditional mop with "accessible" in 1893 arrives at "delightful" in 2016. Who knows if customers' expectations will be redefined in the "delightful" disrupter, ushering in new consumer purchasing behaviors, as well as other disruptive products, adjacencies, or new business models.

Market segmentation:

The Magna Seating example illustrates segmentation as a technique for outcome-driven innovation and how to uncover where to start disrupting within the *Pattern of Disruptions*. Segment customers (by type) within the pattern (for example: the percentage of customers in each disrupter — starting with "usable"; we already identified this is where disruptions are occurring in the ICE passenger vehicle) then conduct "job mapping", customer interviews, and customer observations. "[Christensen and Raynor] argue that activity-oriented market segmentation is a critical success factor for innovations" (Reinhardt et al. 2011). Traditional marketing segmentation uses demographics, such as gender, age, income, education, and occupation, which steers companies in the wrong direction. None of these demographic segments offer insights into customers' expectations for a product or service. "[Christensen and Raynor] reject common methodologies in which segmentation is conducted through demographics, psychographics, price point or product type, and, instead, they proposed a job-based segmentation method" (Reinhardt et al. 2011). Customers have expectations at their level of experience and bundling their expectations with customers someplace else along the range of experiences leads to "one size fits no one" or "overshooting."

With segmentation by *Pattern of Disruptions* approach, Magna will have diverse insights across the full range of consumers to start to understand customers' expectations. Using the observations from its work, I would process map the current state of driverless legislation by country to identify the unmovable design features. Then I would use the pattern to create a framework by customer type (per country). (Later, I go into detail on how to create experiences for prospective customers see Figure 4.1: *Environments Create Pathways for Prospective Customers*). This is where I would pick up the work Magna started with its seating observations. This can all be managed in roadmaps and generational product plans to develop products timed with legislation and customers' expectations for available seating technologies.

Bringing customers into the early stages of outcome-driven innovations across all types (current, latent, and future) is more challenging for disruptive innovations than incremental innovations, which relies upon existing customers and existing markets to derive insights. Segmenting is particularly challenging in a nascent market with early adopters. "Anticipated and nascent markets are notoriously hard to analyze" (Brown et al. 2017). With the additional guidance of segmentation, the pattern can reveal disruptions in nascent markets. The pattern helps to segment the expectations for each customer type. Assume everyone using the products or services in a nascent market are current lead users or nonconsumer prospective customers. This allows the framework to account for varying degrees of exposure to a product or service. "Lead users" are likely to have established knowledge about the product or service and possibly accept some quirks and shortcomings to be first. Be aware of the potential for biases. Building off of interviews and observations with lead users could be misrepresentative of the early majority, a larger group of customers with a different set of expectations. Similarly, interviews and observations with nonconsumer prospective customers can be unreliable in revealing expectations outside of their needs.

Geoffrey A. Moore defines this dynamic as a "chasm", the expectations gap between "early adopters" and "early majority" (Moore 2014). He warns about drawing inferences from lead users. They could be misaligned with customers' expectations in the "early majority." This is key. Moore explains this landmine in the product lifecycle that derails companies' innovations and how to avoid making this mistake in his book, *Crossing the Chasm* (2014). The work of outcome-driven innovations (job mapping, process maps, observations, and segmentation) can be optimized through the *DICE Theory*.

The work described earlier takes resources, which incumbents likely have more of than new entrants. New entrants will need to invest in partnerships through business or innovation ecosystems to acquire customer insights to challenge incumbents deploying the methods described earlier. If incumbents leverage the resources in the ways previously described, they can continually advance upmarket. The *Pattern of Disruptions* is an inherent upmarket defensive strategy. This is a valuable attribute of *DICE*.

Threat Framing

The outcome-driven innovation methods to achieve disruptive innovation are not a small feat. No longer is it enough to steer an organization towards disruptive innovation and transformational growth. There is more work needed by organizations to leverage the foresight in the *Pattern of Disruptions*. It means perpetually scanning for threats. "Identifying changes in customer preferences is a key competence for recognizing disruptive opportunities and threats" (Reinhardt et al. 2011). This is a vital step in order to awaken an entire organization. Companies need a common language to develop its strategy to position its capabilities. In the case of disruptive innovation, this means giving the organization a new language that frames disruptive innovations and articulates scenarios within contexts of realistic opportunities. Changing mindsets begins, literally, with teaching a new language. Key terms such as "disruptive innovation," "customers' expectations," "digital business model," and "customer experience" must be clearly and consistently defined.

This book gives organizations this language. The *Pattern of Disruptions* anticipates competitive threats and reframes them into opportunities. This is consistent with [Alan Meyer's classic 1982 Administrative Science Quarterly article "Adapting to Environmental Jolts"], the opportunity frame leads to far more adaptive behavior and learning than the "threat frame" (Brown et al. 2017). As companies learn from customers' expectations at each disrupter it informs their tactics and methods. For instance, if customers' expectations have not been redefined by disruptive innovations then there is room for continued sustaining or breakthrough innovations, or the market could remain fragmented with companies disrupting in pockets to serve various customers' expectations, or a company could develop an adjacency product platform that aggregates a majority of customers' expectations into a business model. Leaders can now use the *Pattern of Disruptions* to build awareness and to communicate with stakeholders, mobilizing midlevel managers to act. It means having response teams and resource allocation plans that are deployed by senior management with lucid understandings of the organization's course of action.

Scanning but missing a disrupter in the pattern has consequences, whether it was the result of decisions to forgo a disrupter or mismanagement. A good example of the *Pattern of Disruptions* and missing disrupters is Motorola. It was first to mass-produce the cellphone while it was a nascent market. Motorola was the market-leader in compact size cellphones with improved capabilities. Motorola was focused on sustaining innovations for phones at the "accessible" disrupter, making them sleek, stylish, and compact.

> Motorola's dominance of the category seemed all but assured with its 1996 launch of the clam-shaped StarTAC. At five cubic inches and 3.1 ounces, it was the smallest, lightest cell phone in existence. And it was so stylish that supermodels carried it as a runway accessory, and rap artists immortalized it in song. Even with a price tag of $1,100, it was the "must-have" gadget of the fashion elite. (Buchanan et al. 2007)

Meanwhile, the Digital Revolution was shifting the cellphone market from analog to digital, unlocking call quality. Motorola was the analog technology leader in cellphone and slow to digital. Nokia, a European manufacturer, took advantage of digital; it was the standard in Europe. Nokia used digital to disrupt the market at "dependable." Nokia went on to create smaller digital phones, which absorbed Motorola's "accessible" disrupter. Nokia redefined customers' expectations for compact phones taking the market away from Motorola. Nokia continued moving upmarket. When distracted driving became a public policy safety concern, Nokia was one of the first to respond to a major wireless carrier's request for handheld cellphone manufacturers to display a reminder message on the screen. This is the "reliable" disrupter: infrastructure safety (assets) and digital networks (data).

By 2003 other manufacturers had introduced phones. Motorola was under pressure to regain lost market share. It developed the Motorola's RAZR in mid-2004. It recorded hundreds of millions of dollars in sales for a short period. Innovations that excite and motivate customers to purchase are not the same as those that disrupt. There is no shame in making money. Once again Motorola missed technology developments. Third-generation (3G) technology enabled high volumes of data, music, and video. It launched a higher-end phone, the KRZR, "to win more status-conscious customers and boost profit margins" (Buchanan et al. 2007). By this time, Motorola had missed the "dependable" and "reliable" disrupters. At this point, Motorola was no longer innovating along the trajectory that included new insights, redefined by customers' expectations. It was not serving these customers; therefore, visibility to the next disrupters was out of its vantage point. Losing visibility is potentially the greatest derailment of disruptive innovations within the pattern. "Usable" is where smartphones were disrupted by the iPhone.

Motorola fell into the 'dilemma' Christensen identified in his original theory, and this explains why it missed several disrupters. "There is no innovation without failure, and no failure without innovation," says Paul Iske, Founder of the Institute of Brilliant Failures. "And there is a huge difference between people failing through stupidity and failing because they had a brilliant idea whose timing or circumstances were wrong" (Corkindale 2007). Needless to say, a company missing a disrupter (or a series of disrupters) in the pattern only means getting another chance at disruption is harder because those new customer expectations that are driving changes in consumer purchasing behaviors will not be obvious. They will be the result of insights the company missed. Customers exiting will not be enough to explain why.

Strategies

"The problem with conflating a disruptive innovation with any breakthrough that changes an industry's competitive patterns is that different types of innovation require different strategic approaches" (Christensen et al. 2015). I will outline several popular strategy approaches—none of them are a perfect fit. "If your innovation strategy is struggling or failing, consider whether it's because you've locked yourself into a single approach. There are always new problems to solve; learn to apply the solution that best fits your current problem" (Satell 2017). Consequently, instead of picking a strategic approach, I will define the critical decision framework for the integrated choices any company needs to make in order to build a strategy based on *DICE—market entry-points:* (1) to grow through disruptive innovation in products and services (redefining customers' expectations and changing consumers' purchasing behaviors), (2) to transition with sustaining innovations to expand the existing market in a highly turbulent competitive zone, and/or (3) to grow through business model innovation, creating new consumers from nonconsumption. Earlier in this book, I presented and explained the key elements of *DICE* (Figure 2.1). You will need to refresh your understanding of this figure in order to appreciate the maneuverability of the incumbent and the entrant to make strategic decisions because the elements are not shown. In Figure 3.1, I illustrate the implications of the aforementioned market entry-points on strategic choices in the *DICE* model.

- In (1) disruptive innovation is focused on products and services; it favors the capabilities of incumbents sustaining innovation having access to intimate customer knowledge.
- In (2) the potential to be disruptive with products, services, or business models is lost in the turbulence of survival; it is a defensive position.
- In (3) a product or service must first exist before business model innovation can be disruptive; it favors the disruptive capabilities of digital natives and digitally-enabled new market entrants, as digital expands the marketplace for products and services by enhancing user experience and creating network effects.

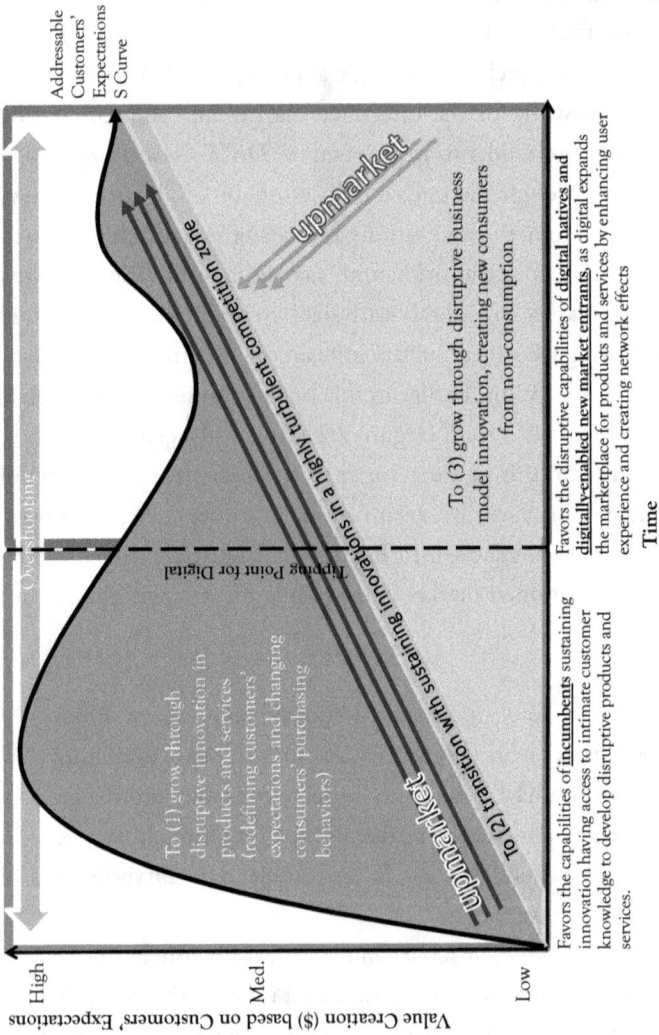

Figure 3.1 Disruptive Innovation Customers' Expectations, emphasis on market entry points

The shading (colors) under the "Addressable Customers' Expectations S Curve" in Figure 3.1 are directional to illustrate a few points: value creation ($) customers' expectations starts out weighted towards products/ services (dark green or dark grey) during the "accessible" and "dependable" disrupters in the *Pattern of Disruptions*, but over time value creation ($) customers' expectations shifts to business models (medium blue or light grey) as a larger portion of value creation ($) customers' expectations. The medium grey diagonal section indicates where customers' expectations are not fully met by products/services or business models; therefore competition is high.

Now consider the implications on the *DICE* model on the three market entry-points. This is where the intersection of disruptive innovation and digital transformation solidify their partnership as the 21st-century's new growth engines. Three key insights emerge.

Value creation can be split into thirds, using the *Pattern of Disruptions*:

1. The first third is between "accessible" and "dependable" disrupters. Value is primarily delivered through products and services.
2. The middle third is between "reliable" and "usable." It is generated from technology and digitally enabled products and services. In this third, we start to see the growing impacts of business models (including digital platform business models). This is where critical decisions are made on digital transformation. If product and service companies miss this digital tipping point—to integrate technology— then their products and services concede value creation to an outside business model creator (including digital platform business models). When this happens these products and services become commodities. Furthermore, network effects from platforms make it unlikely that these same product and service companies can fight back the lopsided value relationship that favors the business model. I illustrated this crucial market entry point of products, services, and business models being disrupted simultaneously through innovations in this critical middle third with an example of the automotive passenger vehicle market and ride-hailing/ridesharing business models in Chapter 2.
3. The latter third of value creation is through business models in "delightful" and networked ecosystems in "meaningfulness". This is

where value from isolated technologies and basic digitization of products and services have nearly maxed out.

No company can manage the resources and capabilities needed to execute on all three strategic choices. Therefore, decisions must be made. Companies absolutely must be capable of leveraging disruption and digital in both dimensions: products/services and business models. However, they must be mindful not to straddle the line between them—partially disrupting in both. This is the only unsustainable pathway, remaining in strategic choice (2) "transitioning with sustaining innovations." "Pulling back to focus on your best customers or on delivering higher quality or a lower price will buy you only a little time, if any" (Downes et al. 2015). Christensen also warned that complacency has an adverse effect on companies. It blinds them to disruptions coming at them from all sides. The three choices do not preclude companies from having other strategy approaches and executing. These are up to the company. Companies must adapt their strategies to fit the problem and the environment. This requires companies to remain focused on deploying resources effectively and to avoid unnecessary distractions that strain resources.

Jeff Bezos (Amazon.com CEO) advised, "It helps to base your strategy on things that won't change" (Kirby et al. 2007). *DICE* anchors the strategic choices, as well as offers pathways for companies to navigate multiple strategies. It defines which market-entry point aligns with products, services, and business models. It offers guidance on where to start your outcome-drive innovation methods to reveal customers' expectations, redefine them with disruptive innovations that ultimately lead to changing consumer purchasing behaviors. It explains how a company can be leading disruption in its sustaining business while creating a new business model to reach non-consumers. This requires the ability to manage separate and often unfamiliar environments alongside a constant flux of changes. The *Pattern of Disruptions* in *DICE* offers the option of "a permanent activity without permanent structures or processes" (Nunes et al. 2011). Consequently, I will recommend several strategic frameworks for disruptive innovation in order to balance the needs of core business strategy and disruptive innovation strategy. Satell (2017) agrees with the need for flexibility in innovation strategies. Satell (2017) remarked, "I found that every innovation strategy fails eventually, because innovation is, at its core, about solving problems—and there are as many ways to innovate as there are types of problems to solve."

Henry Mintzberg and Joseph Lampel summarized the ten schools of strategy processes in "Reflecting on the Strategy Process" (1999). Of those ten, the process that best accommodates the dynamic environmental scanning necessary for the *Pattern of Disruptions*, as well as positions a company's internal capabilities to match external competitive threats, is Michael Porter's *Five Forces* positioning framework. It is highly respected in the business literature and commonly referenced by business leaders. Porter's 1979 *Harvard Business Review* article is as relevant today as it was then. Porter's strategic framework is best situated for incumbents in established markets. The *Five Forces* are modestly incompatible with disruptive innovation. Porter acknowledged the challenge; "managers face a high level of uncertainty about the needs of customers, the products and services that will prove to be the most desired, and the best configuration of activities and technologies to deliver them" (Porter 1996). However, the fundamentals of Porter's framework can offer a recognizable starting point for businesses to build upon for disruptive innovation. Here are Porter's *Five Forces* contextualized for disruptive innovation:

1. "Rivalry Among Existing Competitors" to maintain a focus on core customers' experiences to reveal shifts in customers' expectations.
2. "Bargaining Power of Buyers" to understand consumers have access to networks of information.
3. "Threat of Substitute Products or Services" to recognize the potential for alternatives to conceal nonconsumer purchasing behaviors.
4. "Bargaining Power of Suppliers" to build external capabilities with partners through business models and ecosystems.
5. "Threat of New Entrants" new entrants do not need to develop disruptive products or services. They can leverage incumbents' existing disruptive products or services with business model innovation.

There is another philosophy on strategic thinking, with origins in incremental innovations that is worthwhile repurposing for disruptive innovation. A.G. Lafley and Roger L. Martin authors of *Playing to Win* (2013) defined strategy as "an integrated set of choices that uniquely positions an organization to create sustainable advantage and superior value relative to the competition." The strategic thinking, framework, and guidance Lafley offers is impactful when a decision must be made to maneuver within the *Pattern of Disruption*. Lafley's book draws the most insights for companies based on the key pillars in strategic thinking: "sustainable advantage and superior value relative to the competition."

In addition to the two strategy references (*Five Forces* and *Playing to Win*), there are other "conventional strategies like strategic roadmapping, traditional R&D labs, and using acquisitions to bring new resources and skill sets into the organization" (Nunes et al. 2011) that can be repurposed for disruptive innovation strategy. It just takes context and insights. Building a portfolio of options for specific problems is better than a list for specific tasks that do not meet the challenges. In order for companies to reposition and transform their businesses for new growth opportunities, they "must supplement their traditional approaches with a parallel strategy process that brings the edges of the market and the edges of the organization to the center" (Nunes et al. 2011). The *DICE Theory* gives companies the framework to run parallel strategies. It allows companies to monitor and to detect disruptions to make informed decisions across the innovation portfolio.

There is another adaptive strategy tactic companies can leverage. An article in *Harvard Business Review*, "New Market Conundrum" (2019), described a mimicking of skills or borrowing that new entrants use when entering a new market, as a strategic approach to uncertainty. The intentions behind this tactic are to learn by offering "good enough" alternatives. There is value in acknowledging that a "minimum" is the minimum because it is "good enough." The obvious next steps, I would suggest, are for these companies to learn from their new-market customers, accelerate their intelligence efforts to better understand customers' expectations through customer interviews, customer observations, and testing with rapid prototypes, using trial and error 'play'. At a minimum, as the entrants gain new customers, they should conduct interviews. They are a means to gage if current customers are being "over served", that is, a company's offering surpasses expectations and more developments along the performance trajectory will not likely lead to a higher price point. This is the only way for companies to move upmarket with basic learning from mimicking and to challenge with their own disruptive innovations. In the next section, I discuss saturation-levels and the "Addressable Customers' Expectations" S curve, as well as maneuvering within the *DICE* model in order to be intentional with strategic choices and approaches.

Stay Ahead of the Curve

The *DICE* model sets some limits to analyze saturation levels. Saturation levels are the points in a disruptive opportunity where current customers are satisfied—uninterested in products or services offering increased performance or other improvements (Reinhardt et al. 2011). The model denotes the saturation level with the "Addressable Customers' Expectations" S curve in Figures 2.1; 3.1; and 3.2. It is the highest point where customers' expectations are met by a disruptive innovation offered by a company. Although it is ideal for a company to align its innovation S curve to the addressable S curve, it is extremely demanding. Therefore, it is unlikely that a company's innovations can perfectly align with the addressable S curve.

Paul Nunes described in his book, *Jumping the S Curve,* high performing companies having dual maneuverability along the financial S curve, where they are participating in multiple markets (Nunes et al. 2011). They are successful at managing multiple businesses along different S curves. The maneuvers Nunes described are slightly different than the *DICE* model and its *Pattern of Disruptions* because it is not a business entity companies are managing along the S curve. It is an innovation S curve. Nevertheless, the concept of multiple maneuvers and strategic choices is a powerful approach. In the pattern, companies are managing to the innovation S curve across multiple products, services, business models (digital platforms). The strategic choices a company makes impact how many disrupters (*Pattern of Disruptions)* it participates in and when or if it 'climbs' with a curve (market expansion) or 'jumps' a curve (market creation). A company's abilities to manage multiple innovation S curves depends on its capabilities, talent, and competitors within each disrupter. These are hidden dimensions. Nunes reaches the same conclusion in an article he wrote with Tim Breene (*Reinvent Your Business Before It's Too Late*, 2011):

In our research, we've found that the companies that successfully reinvent themselves have one trait in common. They tend
to broaden their focus beyond the financial S curve and manage
to three much shorter but vitally important hidden S curves—
tracking the basis of competition in their industry, renewing their
capabilities, and nurturing a ready supply of talent. In essence,
they turn conventional wisdom on its head and learn to focus on
fixing what doesn't yet appear to be broken.

Pattern of Disruptions is a dynamic environment, where a company's
capabilities, talents, and competitors influence the disruptive opportunities. Rogers' (2016) theory of disruptive innovation, as a two-sided business model for existing markets, offers evidence that he too considered
multiple maneuvers for disruptive innovations. They are not identical to
the maneuvers in *DICE* and its pattern (Figure 3.2) outlined as follows,
but there are three overlapping similarities that I capture from Rogers
enclosed in brackets. (Note: the letters in the following labels are not
indicative of an order or alignment with a strategy):

- Label "A": A company could expand within a disrupter,
  leaving very little market share available for competitors.
  [*Landside*: "the disrupter quickly takes over the entire market,
  pushing the incumbent into obscurity" (Rogers 2016)].
- Label "B": A company can climb a curve to the top and then
  jump into the next curve.
- Label "C": A company could recognize an upcoming shift
  in customers' expectations, climb with the market expansion
  before realizing its capabilities are unmatched for the climb.
  The company jumps to the next curve.
- Label "D": A company could jump early in preparation
  for building its talent to climb the next curve, realizing the
  market is saturated. [*Splitting the market*: "with the disrupter's
  and the incumbent's business models each taking large shares"
  (Rogers 2016)].

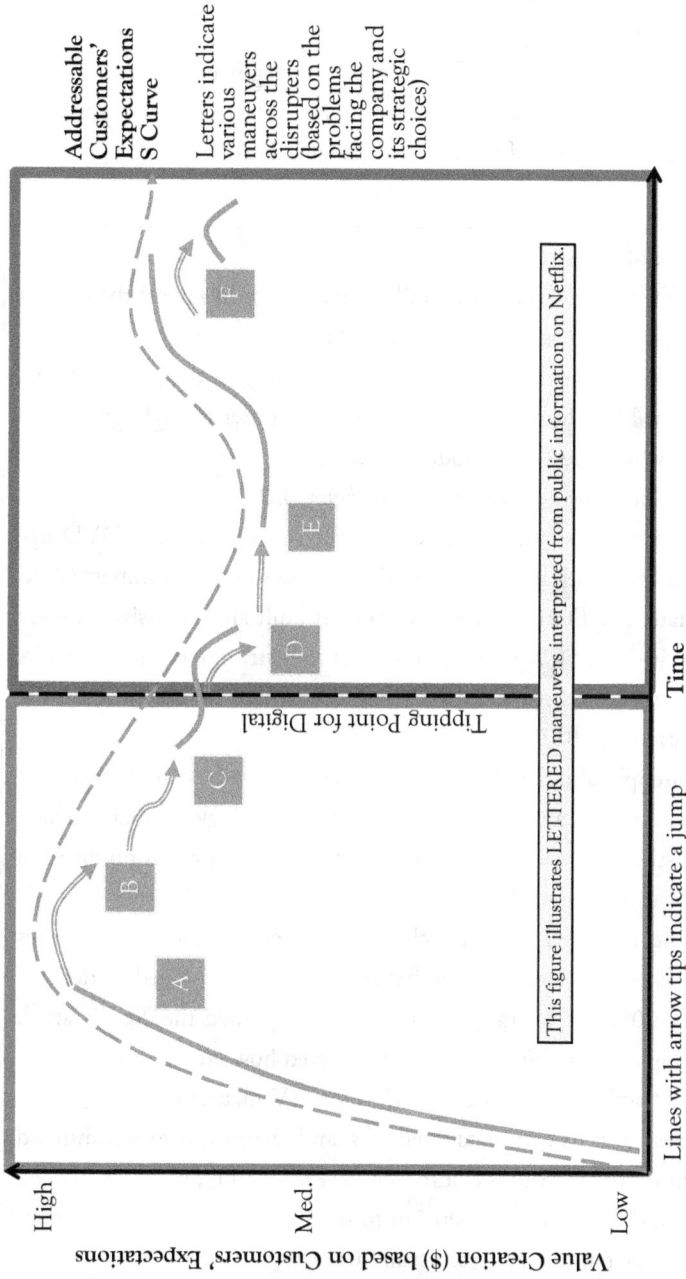

Addressable Customers' Expectations S Curve

Letters indicate various maneuvers across the disrupters (based on the problems facing the company and its strategic choices)

Tipping Point for Digital

This figure illustrates LETTERED maneuvers interpreted from public information on Netflix.

Lines with arrow tips indicate a jump

Time

Value Creation ($) based on Customers' Expectations

High

Med.

Low

Figure 3.2 Disruptive Innovation Customers' Expectations model jumping and climbing S curves—Example Netflix

- Label "E": A company might jump and "pause" before climbing—realizing it needs additional capabilities through partnerships.
- Label "F": A company participates in a segment of the market. [*Niche* "where the disrupter is attractive to only a very specific portion of the market" (Rogers 2016)].

Example of Maneuvers: Netflix

Some of the key decisions by Netflix can be mapped against the *Pattern of Disruptions*. It is very interesting. However, there are many case studies that readers can use to practice mapping to the pattern. Consequently, I will forgo doing this exercise in order to highlight some ways in which the *DICE* model could explain its maneuvers.

Note: follow along with maneuvers in Figure 3.2.

Example of Label A: "it started in 1997 as a mail-order DVD-by-Mail business with monthly subscription fees so that consumers could avoid late fees. During the first decade, it built an impressive logistics chain with over 50 regional warehouses to distribute the DVDs to its customers. By February 2007, it had distributed its billionth DVD" (Venkatraman 2017).

Example of Label B: "Research company Ampere Analysis provided *Business Insider* with data that shows how Netflix's global market share of over-the-top video subscriptions has fallen from a whopping 91% in 2007 to 19% in 2019" (Clark 2020).

Example of Label C: "The classic management textbook theories would have predicted that Netflix should have now failed. Indeed in January 2007, JP Morgan [Securities] downgraded the Netflix stock citing high competition and most wondered how Netflix might create a 'second act' beyond DVD Distribution" (Venkatraman 2017). Netflix invested in its own data, analytics, and algorithms to recommend content to its subscribers (Plummer 2017). By 2007, Netflix launched a million dollar prize competition to improve its recommendation algorithms by ten-percent (Johnston 2017).

Example of Label D: In 2007, Netflix jumped into video streaming (Igbal 2020).

Example of Label E: According to a 2015 video interview of Eva Tse, Director, Big Data Platform at Netflix (posted on to YouTube), in 2009 Netflix was in a data center, but it knew it wanted "to build a global Internet television service" ("Netflix Delivers Billions of Hours of Content Globally by Running on AWS", 2015). Netflix migrated to the cloud, using Amazon Web Services (AWS).

Example Label F: In 2012, Netflix added original content (Igbal 2020). "In late 2012, Netflix signed an exclusive licensing deal with Disney, through which it gained streaming rights to all Disney theatrically released films starting in 2016" (Team 2016). In 2017, Disney left the partnership to create Disney Plus (Kastrenakes 2017). "Days after Disney launched its streaming service, Netflix announced a multiyear partnership with Nickelodeon. The partnership will produce original animated films and television series based on existing Nickelodeon characters and all-new ideas, according to a statement from Netflix" (Brookbank 2019). This builds off of Netflix's competency in developing original content, which could be complemented by its first-ever acquisition, Millarworld, Mark Millar's comic book publishing house (Gartenberg 2017).

Throughout this trapeze act of jumping and climbing competitors must follow and match a company's capabilities and talent. As long as the company continues upmarket, redefining customers' expectations at each consecutive disrupter, it can exhaust the resources of many competitors, crippling efforts to mimic its capabilities, and frustrating outsiders' efforts to capture value through business model innovation. Any company that fails to timely transition between the disrupters could fall into the grey area of "transitioning", a highly turbulent competition zone with sustaining innovations, or stall. "As Matthew S. Olson and Derek van Bever demonstrate in their book *Stall Points*, once a company runs up against a major stall in its growth, it has less than a 10% chance of ever fully recovering" (Nunes et al. 2011). It also means losing connections with customers. Reengaging with a lost customer-base while catching up to competitors' capabilities is expensive and challenging. In the meantime, new entrants could threaten the company with lower pricing and innovative business models.

Key Takeaways From Chapter 3

- The work of outcome-driven innovations (job mapping, process maps, observations, and segmentation) can be optimized through the *DICE Theory*.
- *DICE* helps companies reinterpret existing sustaining business strategy frameworks and repurposing established R&D tools.
- *DICE* maps out the market entry points along with the strategic choices.
- *DICE* describes the innovation S curve, saturation level, and potential maneuvers.
- The *Pattern of Disruptions* is powerful. It can identify the starting point for the next category of customers' expectations ripe for innovations and can identify the place to disrupt next. As companies learn from customers' expectations at each disrupter, it informs their tactics and methods.
- *Part 2: It's the Framework* is complete.

PART III

It's Mastery

CHAPTER 4

Data in the Hands of Many

The *Disruptive Innovation Customers' Expectations* (*DICE*) model and theory provides business leaders with tremendous amounts of guidance to identify and to target new growth in the 21st-century with disruptive innovation and digital transformation: models, strategies, tactics, frameworks, methods, and approaches. Unfortunately, it cannot generate customer data. Investing in a data acquisition strategy is completely in the hands of business leaders. Digital transformation is the business renovation that allows data and technology to inform decisions and to generate business outcomes. Without digital transformation, machine learning, data-enabled learning, edge-computing, and predictive analytics are impossible. Without digital transformation, the data from all of the digital products, technology integrated products and services, or digital platforms for value networks cannot be unlocked. This is where digital transformation brings its greatest value to disruptive innovation.

Digital is a key element in *DICE*. It is the driver behind 4-of-6 disrupters in the *Pattern of Disruptions*. Although *DICE* does not generate data, it does not ignore it. Through its pattern *DICE* helps companies understand data and how to use data. In June 2011, a research paper was published in *Springer*, "Enabling disruptive innovations through the use of customer analysis methods" by Ronny Reinhardt and Sebastian Gurtner. It assessed eight customer analysis methods (Umbrella Methodology, Empathic Design, Lead User, Probe & Learn, Consumer Idealized Design, Information Acceleration, Conjoint Analysis, Job-to-be-done Approach) across 10 research questions (RQ), and evaluated them similar to the Delphi qualitative method. Of the 8-customer analysis methods, the researchers scored the "Job-to-be-done Approach" highest, using a scale of 0-percent "Neither addresses the attribute nor has the potential to address the attribute"; 50-percent "Weakly addresses the attribute or has the potential to address the attribute"; "The Job-to-be-done" Approach received the highest total score." and 100-percent "Explicitly address the attribute or has an extraordinary potential to address the attribute." "The Job-to-be-done" Approach received the highest total score. The primary assumptions behind this approach are: customers 'hire' products and services to meet a need 'a job'——, and they are focused on creating value (benefits) for themselves. "Theory of Jobs to Be Done" was proposed by Christensen and Raynor (2003) in *The Innovator's Solution* and later developed by Christensen in his book, *Competing Against Luck: The Story of Innovation and Customer Choice* (Christensen et al. 2016). It originated in the mid-1990s from his interactions with two consultants from Detroit looking to meet with Christensen to learn about his original theory of disruptive innovation. Through discussions with the consultants Christensen realized that his theory was insufficient "to provide a roadmap for their clients" (Christensen et al. 2016). This perplexed Christensen. He changed his perspective on the problem facing the consultants—from defending an established company (original theory of disruption) to "creating exactly the right product and service", a jobs theory (Christensen et al. 2016). The method and the approach matter to the outcome.

"If inadequate methods of customer analysis and customer orientation are applied, the '*Innovator's Dilemma*' will take its course" (Reinhardt et al. 2011). I heed this advice by embedding the method for customer analysis within the *Pattern of Disruptions*. The customer analysis method is the major categories of customers' expectations. The following table gives readers a relative appreciation for *DICE* and its *Pattern of Disruptions*' customer analysis approach when compared to "Job-to-be-done Approach" and the ways in which the pattern overcome its shortcomings. Without the benefits of the same experts' inputs and based solely on the research paper, I compared the *Pattern of Disruptions* to the "Job-to-be-done Approach" in areas where the researchers scored it less than 100-percent (Table 4.1):

Table 4.1 Summary comparisons of select research questions on customer analysis methods

Research questions (where the "Job-to-be-done Approach" scored less than 100-percent)	Major categories of customers' expectations—Pattern of Disruptions (author's evaluation)
RQ (1c) "Future" Customer Needs—scored 50-percent	Although, customers' expectations evolve over time; the categories to consider the "jobs-to-be-done" do not change; therefore the categories can guide companies to disruptive innovations for future customers.
RQ 2 "Environmental Impact"—scored 0 percent	The *Pattern of Disruptions* specifies customers' expectations that are relevant despite changes in environmental impacts.
RQ 4 "Preference Shift"—scored 50-percent	The "Addressable Customers' Expectations S curve" links customers' expectations and value creation to willingness to pay.
RQ 5 "Saturation Levels"—scored 0-percent	The "Addressable Customers' Expectations S curve" denotes the limitations for saturation levels.
RQ 7 "Emerging Drivers"—scored 0-percent	The patterns are lenses for companies to view emerging drivers.
RQ 8 "Multiple Emerging Markets"—scored 0-percent	The patterns simplify tracking multiple emerging markets and technologies by identifying the key categories of customers' expectations to monitor.
RQ 9 "Non-Consumption"— scored 0-percent	A great deal of the customer insights from sustaining innovations can be leveraged—mainly to establish a baseline for expectations that can be used by a company to understand nonconsumption. In the absence of customer insights, the patterns identify where to investigate unmet needs.
RQ 10 "Barriers to Consumption"— scored 0-percent	"Accessible" is specifically called out in the patterns, as breaking down barriers to ownership/consumption.

A Customer Analysis Method Is Key to Data Strategy

All customer analysis methods demand accurate customer data. However, companies must go beyond data accuracy in order to reveal insights needed to be disrupters. Companies must also consider the myriad of ways data is captured. The data capture process is even more complex within the digital customer acquisition process, where the user experience starts online, adding a new set of challenges for many companies.

The more customers you have, the more data you can gather, and that data, when analyzed with machine-learning tools, allows you to offer a better product that attracts more customers. You can then collect even more data and eventually marginalize your competitors in the same way that businesses with sizable network effects do. Or so the thinking goes. (Hagiu et al. 2019)

This is the data acquisition cycle described by Andrei Hagiu and Julian Wright in their article on defensible data-enabled learning for incremental innovations (Hagiu et al. 2019). Companies must push back against the assumption that more customers create the types of data that creates valuable data for all customers. The first lesson is "Understand It": it is not enough for companies to have customer data, having it does not lead to a profound advantage. Not all data is universally significant and gathering more of it does not transform it into insights. The second lesson is "How to Use It": data becomes valuable because of how it is used. Having lots of data could lead companies to avoid seeking to understand the expectations behind it. This is a serious challenge facing most companies. They will need to learn the value of using data to unlock new growth opportunities. Below I break down the lessons: "Understand It" and "How to Use It".

Understand It:

Rogers describes a paradigm, called *Customer Network Model*, where "current and potential customers have access to a wide variety of digital platforms that allow them to interact, publish, broadcast, and innovate—and thereby shape brands, reputations, and markets" (Rogers 2016). This disrupts traditional marketing tools (mass-communication, mass-promotion, and mass-media) accustomed to many companies. Broadcasting a set of product features, functions, and performance ranges to customers with hopes that those data points will resonate with their needs and expectations is an expensive experiment to test. Nevertheless, this is how many companies interact with their customers. Unfortunately, this is in direct conflict with connected consumers. "Seventy-five percent of customers expect companies to use new technologies to create better experiences," reported by Vala Afshar (*ZDnet.com* 2019). A company's understanding of its customers is complicated by the availability of information, price comparison tools, reviews, and *YouTube* instruction videos. It means customers are not reaching out to companies in the evaluation phase of their buying decisions. Search engines, review aggregators, and social media platforms likely know more about the start of customers' interests than the manufacturers and providers of products and services.

Fortunately, companies with the right capabilities can engage with customers through Internet of Things (IoT) devices, applications, and platforms. "The 2015 Accenture Digital Consumer Survey found that by 2020, nearly half of consumers will own a connected Internet of Things (IoT) device, with strongest demand for home cameras and security, smart watches and fitness devices" (*World Economic Forum* 2015). IoT platforms enable these applications to communicate and to transmit across a spectrum of connected users, devices, and systems as well as a broader networked ecosystem. Billions of Internet-Of-Things (IoT) devices that connect products and services also collect vast amounts of information on customers, as well as usage patterns (see Table 4.2. for five categories of IoT devices). "After machine-learning algorithms analyze this "digital exhaust," a company's offerings can be automatically adjusted to reflect the findings and even tailored to individuals" (Hagui et al. 2019). This data can be used across digital products, services, and business models to serve a market with economies-of-scale and economies-of-scope, as well as to achieve valuable network effects.

Table 4.2 IoT applications: five categories

Presently IoT applications can be grouped into these five categories (Maayan 2020):
1. Consumer IoT—such as light fixtures, home appliances, and voice assistance for the elderly
2. Commercial IoT—applications of IoT in the healthcare and transport industries, such as smart pacemakers, monitoring systems, and vehicle-to-vehicle communication (V2V)
3. Industrial Internet of Things (IIoT)—includes digital control systems, statistical evaluation, smart agriculture, and industrial big data
4. Infrastructure IoT—enables the connectivity of smart cities through the use of infrastructure sensors, management systems, and user-friendly user apps
5. Military Things (IoMT)—application of IoT technologies in the military field, such as robots for surveillance and human-wearable biometrics for combat

In the Digital Age "empowered by digital tools and extensive peer-reviewed knowledge about products and services" (de Jong et al. 2015) companies must be capable of 'speaking' through a broad set of digital tools (e.g. products embedded with intelligence from sensors and predictive analytics software, and AI machine learning algorithms). Customers are not waiting on companies to realize their wants, needs, and frustrations. Customers "often do a better job of choosing among buying options than companies do" (de Jong et al. 2015), which results in customers 'self-selecting' (customers interact with companies based on their preferences: transaction methods, logistics options, and other choices without informing the company of the reasoning behind their behavior). Unfortunately, some companies are being swept up in the tsunami of data.

The *Pattern Of Disruptions* offers some insights into ways companies can better use their data. Insights can be used to assess nonconsumer data, to build assumptions, to test hypotheses, and to pilot projects. Unarticulated needs require companies to use a broad set of tools to analyze customer data, translating unique insights into innovations. A critical component of *DICE* is its *Pattern of Disruptions'* abilities to create an effective customer analysis method, as well as to consider environmental factors, preferences, and emerging drivers, all within its category definitions.

How to Use It:

Based on the work by Reinhardt, an effective customer analysis method informs the types of information, data, and insights needed. "After you've uncovered and understood the job, you need to translate those insights into a blueprint to guide the development of products and services that customers will love" (Christensen et al. 2016). The *Pattern of Disruptions* inform companies on the types of information, data, and insights needed in these ways: where in the pattern are customers' expectations presently, where are customers' expectations focused in the future, what are the products, services, or business models presently available (including alternatives and substitutions), and where have customers' expectations been redefined to create new value and to change consumers' purchasing behaviors (in other words "disrupted"), who are the competitors, capabilities and talent operating in the pattern, and how to identify consumers base on their customer type (current, latent, future). In this case, viewing current customer data through the lens of "why" to build assumptions for nonconsumers could create a starting point for disruptive innovation. To disrupt, companies should use current customer data to establish a baseline for expectations that can be used to understand nonconsumption. Companies can harvest theses insights, including data-enabled learning, to bring prospective customers into a customer journey it curates and controls, that is, loyalty loops.

Forbes reported "100 Stats On Digital Transformation And Customer Experience," based on PTC's *Digital Transformation Report*, that highlights: "Consumers who have an emotional connection with a brand have a 306% higher lifetime value" (*Forbes*, 2019). Customer loyalty programs are ways for companies to mass communicate through their brands and deploy mass marketing directly to customers who already chose to buy their products and services. Loyalty loops are traditionally used for branding and marketing of sustaining innovations, not for targeting nonconsumption. This is a missed opportunity. I advise companies to create contextualized experiences or environments to help attract future customers (based on replicated conditions of unmet needs from current customers).

Loyal customers are valuable. "Loyal customers are five times more likely to buy again and four times more likely to refer the brand to family and friends" (*Forbes* 2019). Consequently, companies should take notice. The "consumer decision journey" (CDJ) was attributed to a June 2009 *McKinsey* report, according to Edelman in "Branding in the Digital Age" (*Harvard Business Review* 2010). The authors of that report "developed their model from a study of the purchase decisions of nearly 20,000 consumers across five industries—automobiles, skin care, insurance, consumer electronics, and mobile telecom—and three continents" (Edelman 2010). Their research revealed stages: consider, evaluate, buy, enjoy, advocate, and bond. The "consumer journey" referenced in Figure 4.1 expands upon four of the stages in the "Loyalty Loop": buy, enjoy, advocate, and bond (Edelman et al. 2015) to offer a model for disruptive innovation. Let's call it the "prospective customer decision journey" or "start joining" loop. In Figure 4.1, I demonstrate how environments can be used for future customers and nonconsumers to observe, evaluate, and consider products and services, or start joining in existing loyalty loops.

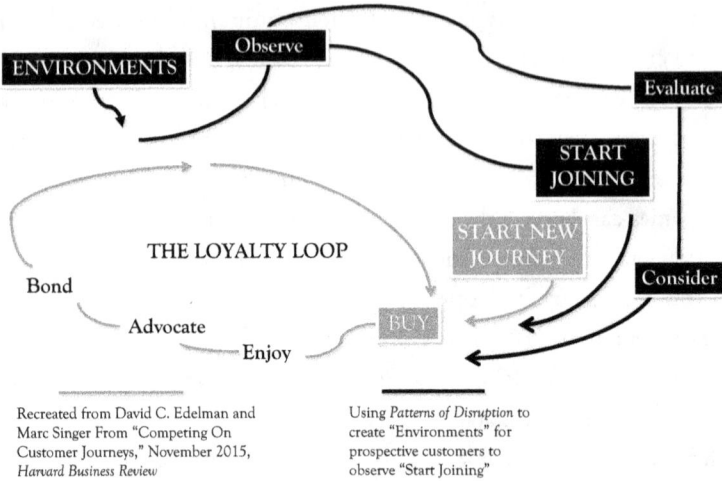

Recreated from David C. Edelman and
Marc Singer From "Competing On
Customer Journeys," November 2015,
Harvard Business Review

Using *Patterns of Disruption* to
create "Environments" for
prospective customers to
observe "Start Joining"

Figure 4.1 Environments create pathways (Note: the text and outlined sections for the "The Loyalty Loop" were inserted to illustrate how "environments" can contribute to "loyalty loops" and to developing the CDJ)

To my knowledge other authors have not developed a process for environments as described in Figure 4.1. Christensen recommended a type of experiential approach: "creating the right set of *experiences* that accompany your product and service in solving the job" (Christensen et al. 2016). The set of *experiences* Christensen described are related to framing a product or service. He illustrates this through the American Girl doll company (now owned by Mattel), which developed experiences around their manufactured dolls. However, this is not the ideal experience for attracting prospective customers, as it requires a purchase. In "Competing on Customer Journey", Edelman gave an excellent example of shaping the customer journey with "environments", using Oakland-based Sungevity—a residential solar panel company that uses Google earth images to illustrate its solar panels on residences and targets homeowners with customized digital marketing, sales, and branding (2015). In the example, Sungevity's CDJ seamlessly enabled a prospective customer to "observe" and to "start joining", bypassing the work customers do on their own to "evaluate" and to "consider." "Rather than merely reacting to the journeys that consumers themselves devise, companies are shaping their paths, leading rather than following" (Edelman et al. 2015). Customers' expectations, using environments to create personalized CDJs (for example: storytelling, social media networks), is an exciting area for emerging technology developments. Augmented reality and virtual reality are excellent technologies to leverage in environments with contextualized experiences. Customers' expectations can help structure CDJs through digital marketing (Social Media, integrate platforms, and brand loyalty).

According to a February 2018 study that surveyed "1,269 business leaders at global enterprises who are responsible for selecting technologies to support [customer experience (CX)] and marketing initiatives and for defining metrics to evaluate success," CX-led businesses outperformed in these metrics: "1.6x higher brand awareness, 1.5x higher employee satisfaction, 1.9x higher average order value, 1.7x higher customer retention, 1.9x return on spend, and 1.6x higher customer satisfaction rates" (*Adobe* 2018). Forester defined an "experience-led company" as "invests in the customer experience across people, processes, and technology" (*Adobe* 2018). It is worthwhile to note that in the United States (USA) pharmaceutical companies have been advertising drugs and treatments direct-to-consumer in television ads since 1985, but the advertising "only really took off in 1997 when the Food and Drug Administration (FDA) eased up on a rule obliging companies to offer a detailed list of side-effects in their infomercials (long format television commercials)" (*Bulletin of the World Health Organization*, 2009). This is an example of companies in the US using environments to describe unmet needs and to attract prospective customers to their products and services.

Quesenberry (2016) offers a "four-step social media framework" that he suggests can help marketers in developing individual solutions. This is how companies can apply the steps to *Pattern of Disruptions*:

- "Define the status quo": If you have current customers, then benchmark their customer expectations to create CDJs based on where they are in the patterns. This is more difficult in nascent markets with a majority of "lead users" or nonconsumption markets. However, using current customer data to glean basic assumptions could be resourceful.

- "Listen to your target audience": Leverage the environment to create opportunities for observation data from surroundings. "Start with simple Google searches on your brand name, analytics tools within social networks, and look to secondary research, such as the Pew Research Internet Project, Nielsen, or Edison Research, to identify large trends in social media use" (Quesenberry 2016). Be mindful of following insights derived from analytics tools within social networks. These networks can reflect intense likes and dislikes not evidenced-based or consistent with a larger majority. "For long-term consumer monitoring, look into a social media monitoring service, such as Radan6 from Salesforce.com, Hootsuite, or Hubspot" (Quesenberry 2016).
- "Create social media content that drives engagement": Facilitate content to "start joining", for example, Sungevity used close-loop hyper-personalized marketing communications and onboarding tactics on prospective customers. This an encouraging example for companies looking to gain data and permissions from customers when the innovation outcomes benefit customers.
- "Optimize it for audiences on your digital channels": Use social media networks and digital channels to share "environments" to guide the CDJ. Proceed with caution, acknowledging the potential for "group think" in social networks.

In addition, develop CDJ pilots of various experience-driven customer expectations within the patterns. Measure key performance indicators (KPIs)—especially for sales (new joiners, new buyers, new viewers of journeys, and new purchases). I highly recommend reading (Edelman 2015) to develop KPIs for CDJ. These new approaches to customer analysis methods focused on customers' expectations and using environments to attract and to promote "start joining" in the CDJ are critical for disruptive innovations. However, without the investments in data and digital transformation (digital channels, social media networks, and digital content) they could go underutilized. "Digital transformation and a focus on customer experience can generate a 20–30% increase in customer satisfaction and economic gains of 20–50%" (*Forbes* 2019).

Digital Transformation: The Tipping Point

According to a 2019 *Forbes* article, "40% of all technology spending in 2019 [went] towards digital transformation. Companies [were forecasted to] spend a total of more than $2 trillion on digital transformation in 2019." Key themes throughout the value propositions for digital transformation is meeting customers' expectations and delivering memorable customer experiences (Rogers 2016). According to a survey of executives: "the top benefits of digital transformation are improved operational efficiency (40%), faster time to market (36%) and the ability to meet customer expectations (35%)" (*Forbes* 2019). This survey data is slightly alarming for innovators seeking new growth because "the ability to meet customer expectations" should be more of a focus if companies are looking to grow from digital transformation investments. "Faster to market" is a consistent business execution priority that is not unique to growth. "Operational efficiency" is primarily a sustaining incremental focus. However, it can be argued that relative to all other business priorities, having customer expectations in the top three is significant.

After reading an interview with the CEO of Duke Energy about industry transformation in *MIT Sloan Management Review* I was reminded of this story that was made possible by a time when large telephone utility companies owned payphones:

My son just received his first smartphone. I decided to test his reactions to a payphone. There is a payphone outside of the public library. I gave him a handful of coins. He decided to call his paternal Grandmother. He inserted the coins into the slot, picked up the handset, and heard a noise (i.e., dial tone). Then he turned to me and asked, "Where do I get the number?" I laughed, mostly at myself for not thinking about the number. I no longer memorize any phone numbers. I reached into my pocket, pulled out my smartphone, and found the number.

I discovered there were lessons for me too from that payphone experiment with my son. And these lessons apply to the digital transformation of a physical business.

Lesson #1: The substance is the same.
Whether my son called his Grandma on a smartphone or a payphone, as long as the telephone number was correct and the line was intact, the call would go through.

Takeaway: Smartphones have numerous benefits over the payphone, but there is one critical piece of information that doesn't change, the substance. The phone number must be correct. If a physical business has the right substance then its digital journey might be less painful.

Lesson #2: Just add technology will not work.
Physical businesses have built-in barriers and pipelines. Many of us understand and tolerate these frustrations, for example, hierarchical approvals, complex contracts, and lengthy agreements.

Takeaway: Technology is absolutely a part of the digital journey. However, it is not the answer to everything. Technology will not "fix" what is wrong with a business, for example, business model, organizational structure, strategy, culture, and talent retention.

Lesson #3: Don't forget the user experience.
While my mother-in-law accepted the call from the comforts of her living room, my son was standing outside, in a public place, holding a personal conversation. After the initial humor of using a payphone wore off, he was ready to hang up.
Takeaway: Just because a business' processes and policies work for it, doesn't mean they work for customers, employees, and partners. Failing to examine the business from the outside-in could lead to creating a digital business that codifies everything stakeholders dislike. It's a missed opportunity.

Interestingly, there is another utility with a long history of managing dynamic external market forces (for example: regulations, legislation, shareholders, public opinion, and emerging technologies) with guidance on physical meets digital transformation. The power and utility industry is experiencing significant market changes driven by renewable energy (for example: wind, solar, and micro-grids) and the direct-to-consumer new customer relationships it created. These insights are from a longer interview by *MIT Sloan Management Review* with the CEO of Duke Energy about industry transformation. "We have to keep up with what customers expect from an experience: information, control, convenience, and choice," says Lynn Good, CEO of Duke Energy Corp (*MIT* 2017). Good described the shift from asset focused (meters) to customers with always-on mobile apps and smart home devices. Customers expect to communicate with a company and not through an asset, in a timely manner. Companies like Duke, which did not traditionally communicate directly with end-users, did not have information systems to manage digital contact information, such as e-mail addresses, or mobile apps to monitor usage. Duke is learning and working through these data and technology gaps.

> Good: Mobile apps are the centerpiece of giving customers access to the data and options they are seeking. And then we are putting new devices on our systems: smart meters, sensing devices, and communication technologies that allow the network to gather and deliver all this information. (*MIT* 2017)

For some industries (chemicals, utilities, agriculture), the ability to meet customers' expectations could be hindered by the unfamiliar nature of the relationships needed to communicate direct-to-consumer. Companies unaccustomed to direct communications with end-users could find that the "one-size-fits-all" methods intended to inform suppliers worsen interactions with end-users. A company with cumbersome outdated digital channels could be devalued by end-users. This could lead to a tarnished reputation and brand, both of which put companies under public scrutiny. These companies could be considered less innovative (Afshar 2019). Digital puts demands on component manufacturers and system integrators, as well. This is a change from the traditional transactional sales pipeline to a data pipeline, through which end-users push their expectations. These companies will need to find new ways to manage customer relationships in a smartphone world, where customers expect large-scale utilities to behave similar to downloadable software, smart devices, and apps. Despite the challenges, digital transformation will increase demands from customer expectations. There are significant gains to be made for those companies who are successful. "Companies that earn $1 billion a year earn an additional $700 million over three years by investing in customer experience" (*Forbes* 2019).

Presently, if a customer has to ask a company for any information that would have been shared previously on invoices, payments, orders, or complaints, then the customer questions if the company is paying attention. "76% of consumers expect companies to understand their needs and expectations" (*Forbes* 2019). Connected customers expect immediate interactions and reactions to data and information. Increased focus on customers' expectations could put pressure on the culture of established companies unaccustomed to digital channels. "70% of digital transformations fail, most often due to resistance from employees" (*Forbes* 2019). Nonetheless, the company's digital transformation must meet these customer expectations. It requires a mindset shift and new roles within these organizations that did not exist in the past. Duke understands the need to bring in talent with backgrounds in customer engagement. "Good: We recently named a chief customer officer from outside the industry, someone who has a background with Disney and United Airlines, to help create the picture for what customer relationships should look like" (*MIT* 2017).

Legacy businesses familiar with navigating external forces may have the upper hand in managing the complexities of digital transformation for incremental innovations. There are tools they can use to leverage their incumbent knowledge. For instance, "discovery-driven planning" (DDP) is a good starting point. It is an iterative product development cycle described by Rita McGrath and Ryan McManus in "Discovery-Driven Digital Transformation" (2020). It was adopted into "the lean startup" tool kit (McGrath et al. 2020). *The Lean Start Up* is the title of Eric Ries' book that explains new product development process with steps (build, measure, and learn) to experiment and to guide the acceleration of products, services, and business models to market. Legacy businesses have resources to deploy "DDP" methods. They can run multiple experiments and pilots to learn fast and to fail fast. These manufacturers and providers offer vital products and services. They already have a reason to engage with end-users. They do not need a gimmick or pitch.

Legacy businesses have survival skills that they can tap into: core understanding of the industry (safety, standards, and best practices), experienced talent in their workforces with relevant knowledge, long-standing relationships with the key players, and established supply bases that cater to their business intricacies and quirks. "Incumbent companies have some great advantages over new competitors: paying customers, financial resources, customer and market data, and larger talent pools" (McGrath et al. 2020). Many have proven their resilience before and they have the scars to prove it.

Incumbents may find comfort in their abilities to survive digital transformation with incremental sustaining innovations. However, too much comfort is the essence of the "dilemma" identified by Christensen in his original *Theory of Disruptive Innovation*. Complacency can lull them into an artificial sense of security. Being an incumbent company with heavily invested assets in an established industry does not better prepare a company to take on disruptive innovation. The professional boxer Michael "Mike" Tyson has some words of caution: "Everybody has a plan until they get punched in the face." For example, Airbnb and Uber transformed hotels and taxicabs leveraging the same business model of large hotel chains and taxi services (McAfee et al. 2017). They used the assets: hotel chains licensed to franchisees or investors, who build and maintain the properties, and taxi services sell medallions to chauffer-licensed drivers, who purchase vehicles configured for operating a sole proprietorship. The key difference in the asset approaches is the use of digital platforms, which eliminated transactional frictions, inconvenience—waiting in bad weather for a taxi, and finding a room or taxi during high utilization periods, and lack of transparency—wondering if the ratings for hotels are accurate or if the taxi driver is friendly. "The rules of the growth game have changed and if you understand and master the new rules, you have a good chance of surviving and thriving as anyone" (Parker et al. 2016).

Digital Disruption Cannot Be Ignored

In the Industrial Era, businesses needed assets (property, land, equipment, and financial resources). These capabilities weighed heavily on the operating model. They do not yield the same advantages for digital. This means a set of new rules. Businesses must undergo a rebalancing of capabilities. Digital transformation offers a reprioritization of capabilities to fill in digital deficiencies. "[A] new technology alone is not enough to propel a business into transformational growth" (Johnson 2018). "[D]igital technologies are rewriting the rules of business" (Rogers 2016). This rewrite is a collision between empowered consumers enabled by technology and the offerings of companies. Companies must translate their investments in digital transformation into value propositions, user experiences, CDJs (including prospective customer journeys), contextualized experiences (or environments), and digital channels to support loyalty loops and start joining that are integrated and hyperpersonal. Otherwise, customers will easily replace a company's products and services with little switching costs because competitors will have seamless onboarding. Advancements in digital technologies have significantly lowered the initial cost of market entry and have made switching from one platform to another much easier. This is why digital disruption cannot be ignored.

An incumbent company can focus on digital to enable sustaining innovation and never direct its focus towards disruptive innovation for transformational new growth. This will lock it into one strategic choice: "transitioning with sustaining innovations in a highly turbulent competitive zone." See Figure 3.1. If the core business needs digital to compete, then why would anyone second-guess needing it for transformational business too? The consequence of not developing digital transformation capabilities could be codifying processes and structures for an organization that cannot adapt. This is likely the worst outcome of digital transformation, where businesses invest in costly restructuring of its digital capabilities—yet fail to gain access to the business outcomes because those insights are further away from the areas where the business was enabled with digital capabilities. They are out of the range of their insights.

Digital transformation will reshape businesses and the next generations of products, services, and business models. Digital is the "tipping point" for many markets. This was described in *Disruptive Innovation Customers' Expectations Model* (Figure 2.1) with the additional disrupters: reliable, usable, dependable, and meaningfulness. For nondigital native companies, digital capabilities unlock these disrupters in the pattern: reliable, usable, dependable, and meaningful. I mentioned this in the previous chapter on maneuvers, but I will restate it: if businesses do not capture the value of digital in its products, services, and business models, then another company (likely an unknown competitor of its products and services) will build digital capabilities through business model innovation on top of their products and services, shifting the value formula away from those products and services—commoditizing them. The unfortunate part of this shift will be the complete blindsiding of business leaders. It will seem like it happened overnight.

Digital transformation capabilities are an investment. Not all of the capabilities will yield an immediate return-on-invested-capital (ROIC). Eventually, some of the digital capabilities companies develop will become the "norm," and the investments companies made will pay off. Unfortunately, which of those digital capabilities will be the "status quo" is yet to be determined. They are being redefined by customers' expectations, changes in purchasing behaviors, and saturation levels. Companies must prepare their leadership for ambidextrous decision-making in a dynamically changing environment. Companies should be proactively involved in ensuring survival during in the 21st-century. It cannot be ignored, and there is no turning back the clock for a do-over.

Key Takeaways From Chapter 4

- A customer analysis method is key to data strategy.
- *DICE* and its *Pattern of Disruptions* address shortcomings found by industry experts in the popular "Job-to-be-done Approach" (based on an assessment of customer analysis methods) to help companies identify the types of information, data, and insights needed to have an effective customer analysis method.
- *DICE* informs data acquisition strategies to empower digital transformation.

- Digital transformation unlocks the value in the digital disrupters in the *Pattern of Disruptions*: reliable, usable, delightful, and meaningfulness.
- Digital transformation requires companies to engage with customers in new ways. "Big data" will continue to be a challenge for companies looking to build customer loyalty—particularly the vast amounts of data and the various methods customers use to self-select.
- Environments can develop connections that companies need in digital customer acquisitions to invite consumers to "start-joining" its loyalty loop without a purchase.
- These three lessons apply to the digital transformation of a physical business; #1: The substance is the same; #2: Just add technology will not work; and #3: Don't forget the user experience.

CHAPTER 5

First-Mover Advantage

Up to this point in the book, based on what has been covered, you might have a renewed confidence in your business and its abilities to grow through disruptive innovation and digital transformation in the 21st-century. A quick recap of the last four chapters:

- Understanding the contributions made to the original theory of disruptive innovation that evolved into *Disruptive Innovation Customers' Expectations Theory*—translating disruptive innovation into a repeating pattern of major categories of customers' expectations that when redefined by new value creation can change consumers purchasing behaviors;
- Digital was previously missed. It is a determinant in 4-of-6 disrupters in the *Pattern of Disruptions*, highlighting the roles digital transformation capabilities play in *DICE*;
- Modeling *DICE's* three dimensions: *Pattern of Disruptions'* products/services and business models—targeting value creation and customer expectations—and the innovation S curve "Addressable Customers' Expectations"—targeting saturation levels. Companies must be prepared to consider these dimensions, which includes navigating market entry points, maneuvering beneath the S curve, and positioning;
- Shifting mindsets toward new ways of market segmentation with a focus on customers' expectations (behaviors) and outcome-driven innovations, using process mapping, jobs mapping, interviews, and observations.

- Playing by the rules of digital (using the *Pattern of Disruptions* to develop customer-analysis methods, data acquisition strategies, and digital transformation capabilities to unlock digital channels, curate social network platforms, create environments for CDJs: "start joining" and loyalty loops);

How much, and how quickly a company can absorb the guidance in this book? These are questions for change management experts. Even without specific insights into an organization's capabilities, I must caution business leaders against overestimating the complexities in the aforementioned points and attempt "first-mover advantage" without a mastery of the organizational competencies needed to manage maneuvers, as well as trialing them with some success.

A key benefit of disruptive innovation and digital transformation are their abilities to create "first-mover advantage" in a variety of circumstances. Applying the research done by Fernando Suarez and Gianvito Lanzolla and presented in their article, "The Half-Truth of First-Mover Advantage" (2005), "based on a thorough examination of the literature on first-mover advantage, as well as an analysis of more than 30 cases of early entry into new product spaces," the authors identified two conditions for "first-mover advantage": "the pace at which the technology of the product in question is evolving and the pace at which the market for that product is expanding." I will suggest ways the *Pattern of Disruptions* can help companies decide on "first-mover advantage." I will use the terms from *Disruptive Innovation Customers' Expectations* model for innovation S-curves: "jumping" (market creation) and "climbing" (market expansion).

Here are some considerations for "climbing" an innovation S curve. Market expansion is the result of unrealized customer demands within existing markets, for example, "value innovation" (*Blue Ocean Strategy* 2005), new brands, or business models. These are market expansion conditions for "climbing" S curves within disrupters:

- Technology adoption is slow;
- Transparency of processes and information is low; and
- Customers' expectations are high.

Industries such as healthcare and utilities are two that are top of mind for "climbing" with "first-mover advantage." It is not to say that companies in other industries would not be successful "climbing" under these conditions. For instance, if a company has a business model that lowers its operating costs while meeting customers' expectations (and its decision to "climb" is preceded by a disciplined assessment) then "first-mover advantage" is a good decision. "Depending on circumstances, such as availability of data and a customer's cooperation, a [company] might build a [customer] value model for an individual customer or for a market segment, drawing on data gathered from several customers in that segment" (Anderson 2014). It requires closely monitoring the investments needed to pivot or to upgrade capabilities.

These are ideal positions for "jumping" into S curves looking to gain "first-mover advantage" with disruptive innovations:

- Technology is evolving; and
- Create new markets from "future" customers (non-consumption); or
- Create new markets from "latent" customers with unrealized needs or frustrations.

Creating new markets that meet and prioritize new customers' expectations across customer types and creating new markets from customers with disparate needs (grouping them together) to pull the market away from alternative products and services are better positions for companies to jump. *Why?* In the absence of defined customers' expectations, companies have a better chance of directing and steering customers toward their products and services. This is fundamental. It means companies will have customer data and insights to (re)define customers' expectations before their competitors. These companies can curate new customers through environments, "start joining," and loyalty loops, which eventually lead to market expansion.

On the opposite side of "first-mover advantage", there are two threats: (1) Companies must overcome their reluctance to place a bet in an area of uncertainty. History is full of stories of companies with technologies and/ or products that met future customers' expectations. These companies arrived early to the market, but they did not take "first-mover advantage." They underestimated the markets, for example, Kodak (digital camera), Blockbuster (video streaming), and Nokia (first built-in camera phone). (2) Capabilities to manage the complexities of the maneuvers needed to be successful for "first-move advantage." Capabilities impact a variety of business decisions: the interactions between partners, the development of platforms and business models, the reactions of customers to new technologies, and the organizational understanding needed to create or to unlock value.

In this chapter, I discuss the complexities of two multinational business and technology enterprises, through the guidance of the two conditions for "first-mover advantage": "the pace at which the technology of the product in question is evolving and the pace at which the market for that product is expanding" (Suarez et al. 2005) and the threats: reluctance to place a bet in an area of uncertainty and managing complex decision-making maneuvers. I use a business case on Siemens for digital transformation. I use a business case on Volkswagen's *Strategy 2018* and "Dieselgate" for a disruptive innovation product. Both examples reflect public information. The goal is not to simplify these cases to fit into the dialogues in this book, or to compress or minimize the business decisions into these pages. The goal is to offer guidance and to reflect on these cases as examples of "first-mover advantage", as they impact the future of digital transformation and disruptive innovation.

I illustrate these points by extracting only the key elements from a 2018 Harvard Business School case study, "Digitalization at Siemens," by David J. Collis and Tonia Junker. I highly recommend reading the entire case study for a more comprehensive perspective. Siemens was not threatened by the need to place a bet on digital transformation. Siemens was the first supplier to offer a "complete lifecycle of products and production facilities"—software and hardware (Collis et al. 2018). It had "first-mover advantage." The S curve maneuvers (impacted by capabilities, talent, and competitors) Siemens made within its digital technology platform led to opportunities for growth, based on interactions with partners, reactions of customers, operating model, and value creation. The time Siemens lost to managing complex decisions to drive maneuvers posed the greatest threat.

Joe Kaeser took over as CEO of Siemens in 2013. He did not think the previous digital initiative went far enough, as it was launched with a small group of Siemens' business units (Collis et al. 2018). He recognized digital needed to be expanded to all businesses. "Kaeser clearly categorized businesses into electrification, automation, and digitalization [EAD] components" (Collis et al. 2018). The new initiative would be driven by EAD. It was "introduced in spring 2014, about the time Siemens implemented the new organizational structure, streamlining divisions" (Collis et al. 2018). Siemens' managing board created the "Siemens Digitalization Program."

"The board discussed whether Siemens should launch a central analytics platform to be used across all divisions to create value from machine-generated data—e.g. for predictive maintenance schemes" (Collis et al. 2018). To avoid potential pushback from business units seeing this as a corporate initiative, "Siemens executives reasoned that Siemens' strategy was based on the specific offerings of the business units" (Collis et al. 2018). So it created a decentralized analytics platform approach—unlike GE's corporate top-down approach (Predix), the more centralized platform of one of its main competitors (Collis et al. 2018). This led to the analytics platform being built as a base to support applications for specific use cases, rather than being designed centrally to support all possible business needs (Collis et al. 2018). Throughout this case I highlight the many times that the platform technology architecture changed. This was possibly a mistake that slowed down Siemens' overall digital transformation. (In Chapter 6 of this book, I examine the necessary intersections needed in an innovation portfolio to capitalize on transformational growth across silos.)

> [A]t the end of 2014 Siemens held a Capital Market Day for analysts. [Chief Technology Officer Siegfried Russwurm, the official leader of Siemens Digitalization Program] presented the digitalization framework with the quantified EAD levers, announcing that under "D" Siemens currently generated €2.4 billion of vertical software and €500 million of digital service revenues from more than 300,000 remotely monitored devices, while enhanced "A" plus related services were a €33 billion business and enhanced "E" accounted for €37 billion of revenue. (Collis et al. 2018)

Prior to the creation of its "Siemens Digitalization Program," building off electrification and automation of power plants, as well as energy power grids, Siemens was primarily focused on being an asset company. "Electrification was a common denominator for all of Siemens' businesses, from power to rail to factory automation," and automation was the "intelligent management and control to the system," noted Siemens Chief Strategy Officer (CSO), Horst J. Kayser (Collis et al. 2018). Digitization offered the potential to unlock growth across the value chain. "The future was in the software above the automation layer, meaning digitalization," noted Kayser. Siemens anticipated combining the physical and virtual aspects of its automation business (Collis et al. 2018).

By this time, Siemens had been on a digital journey for eight years. In 2006, "Anton Huber, responsible at that time for the Automation & Drives business" was being asked by customers for tools to simulate "technically complex plants or processes" (Collis et al. 2018). Huber appealed to Siemens board to acquire UGS, a U.S. Texas-based software player. It was "a step toward digital factories in which virtual factories could be constructed, allowing manufacturers to test out their operations before building even a single physical machine or product, as flight simulators allowed pilots to virtually fly a plane" (Collis et al. 2018). This acquisition transferred capabilities between the two companies: Siemens learned "how to sell software as a license directly to end users, separately from automation sales, which typically went through a value added reseller," and UGS gained access to large contracts "with credibility as part of Siemens" (Collis et al. 2018).

Following the acquisition of UGS, Siemens developed other digital capabilities. According to Roland Busch, CSO in 2008, Siemens had to face digital; it meant change for the whole. "While some divisions, like automation, had already started to make investments for a digital future, the key was for all to realize" (Collis et al. 2018). In 2010, the "2nd IT Revolution Initiative" was launched by Busch initially "with the 15 or so businesses that would be most impacted by digitalization, before extending it more broadly across the portfolio" (Collis et al. 2018). Siemens moved away from its horizontal IT approach to a vertical IT approach with emphasis on "domain-specific expertise, such as fluid dynamics for analyzing liquid flows in pipelines, would be critical to developing successful software applications" (Collis et al. 2018).

There were concerns raised by some Siemens executives "about the reach and the universality of the IoT technology" (Collis et al. 2018). Industrial Internet of Things (IIoT) offered the chance to unleash the value of all of that data, transforming digital—from physical assets—to virtual assets, equipped with decision-making, predictive analytics, and machine learning. "[N]etworked machines could also 'learn' over time how to improve performance as a system" (Collis et al. 2018). Unfortunately, realizing these benefits was a challenge (and not just for Siemens but for all companies). One such barrier was "the lack of technical standards to ensure that all devices from all manufacturers could communicate with one another" (Collis et al. 2018). There were other competing technologies "for connecting everyday objects to networks was radio-frequency identification (RFID), but it was not the only standard, competing with WLAN, Near Field Communication, and Bluetooth" (Collis et al. 2018). Lastly, there were threats to security: "poor encryption of sensitive private information, combined with weak passwords, and defective user interfaces could turn Internet-connected devices into major security risks" (Collis et al. 2018). There will always be uncertainties when a company is transforming its business. The imperative is to manage it.

"Only companies like Siemens, with a heritage and accumulated expertise in that domain, would be successful" (Collis et al. 2018). Siemens also embraced opportunities digital offered for a service business. Admittedly "Busch explained that service had often been treated as an underdog within Siemens, but with digitalization it became strategically more important" (Collis et al. 2018). This meant connecting directly to the "installed base of Siemens equipment at customers' sites" (Collis et al. 2018). This required "a common connectivity tool—the common Remote Service Platform (cRSP)" that was adopted by all of the businesses (Collis et al. 2018). "While all business units could use cRSP, many divisions had built their own data and analytics platforms, with their own names, adapted to their customers' particular needs" (Collis et al. 2018). Head of Strategy Development Gerhard Fohringer explained, "Focus is more important than synergies" (Collis et al. 2018).

Speed and scope are challenges for managing multiple configurations of platforms and data within the same organization. As Busch explained, "Each branch has its own speed and conservatism" (Collis et al. 2018). A decision was made to create a technical base, the foundation for a functioning system, and platform management for it was created in a separate organizational unit. The technical base for the platform would serve as "the common layer" for the business units "to build software add-ons based on their knowledge of their verticals" (Collis et al. 2018). Siemens' Corporate Technology department would become "a corporate organization that could establish and develop a platform" (Collis et al. 2018). "In early 2014, Siemens started Industrial Data Analytics (IDA) as a cross-divisional initiative to build a platform for industry" (Collis et al. 2018). "[B]y mid-2015 IDA was developing the first use cases from energy, mobility, and healthcare" (Collis et al. 2018).

> In contrast was the Digital Factory, Siemens' own business that operated two state-of-the-art factories in Germany and Shanghai at the forefront of digitalization. Their capability to create a "digital twin" of a product, process, or plant allowed for the investigation of the consequences of potential actions or scenarios in a virtual universe that could be used to optimize actions in the physical world. Russwurm described the development: "The digital twin allows for simulating things long before they are built, which speeds up time significantly for our customers. We don't build prototypes anymore but simulate everything, and the first product is really supposed to be a sellable product." (Collis et al. 2018)

Siemens' digital journey was influenced by its operating model (corporate and business units), its digital resources (IT infrastructure), value creation (moving into services), and customer reactions. There were an estimated 12 years between the start of Siemens' digitization journey (2006) and the publishing of the case study (2018). Transforming an asset-focused company to a digital-focused company with a strong customer base and billions of dollars in revenue requires a complex balancing act to maneuver and to alter its course of direction. According to a March

19, 2020 article in the Wall Street Journal, "Chief Executive Joe Kaeser would be replaced by current Deputy CEO Roland Busch by early next year at the latest, cementing the company's shift from a conglomerate into a business more focused on digital transformation" (Bender 2020).

In the case of Volkswagen (VW), the "first-mover advantage" it attempted was through disruptive innovation. I am certain many readers are familiar with the scandal "Dieselgate" that was "the largest corporate fraud in history," a cheating engine technology software code in VW's emissions control computer discovered by West Virginia University graduate school students (Forsgren 2019). Therefore, I will highlight two key aspects of this case that are significant: VW was on the right path to understand customers' expectations, but it was outmaneuvered by the mechanical impossibilities of the innovations, and it resorted to technology to make up the gaps.

According to a case study by National Aeronautics and Space Administration Chief Knowledge Officer, Roger Forsgren, titled "Dieselgate: A Case Study in Engineering Ethics," Volkswagen "left engineers working on the project with an ethical test that they ultimately failed" (Forsgren 2019). It started with VW's goal in 2008 "to become the world's largest automobile company within a decade," according to its "Strategy 2018" (Forsgren 2019). It saw the United States as the market to expand. In order to accomplish its strategic goal, VW had to challenge Toyota for the top spot. VW set its sights on Toyota, specifically taking share away from its "fuel-efficient line of hybrid vehicles that were becoming increasingly popular in the lucrative U.S. market" (Forsgren 2019). There was one major weakness with hybrids and that is their poor power and acceleration performance.

VW placed big bets on market creation in the United States with clean emissions and with no loss in engine performance (power and acceleration). According to Forsgren, this put forth "unrealistic—and perhaps impossible—goals set by the automaker to simultaneously push engine power levels up and emission levels down" (2019). VW would build off of its diesel engine technology, which was very popular in Europe and less popular in the United States. VW's diesel engine technology had a tradeoff. It had less carbon dioxide (CO_2) emissions and more nitrogen oxide (NO_x) emissions. CO_2 was more of a focus in Europe's efforts to combat climate change, and NO_x emissions were more of the focus to combat poor air quality in the United States by the Environmental Protective Agency (EPA) and by the California Air Resource Board (CARB). The decision-making threat to "first-mover advantage" for VW was the same as Siemens for completely different reasons. Considering it was impossible to meet U.S. customers' expectations for vehicles with clean engine technology that did not sacrifice power and acceleration performance, VW sold an unrealistic target as disruptive innovation. This knowledge did not factor in the decision to proceed with the strategy and vehicle development. There were no maneuvers available to VW. *DICE* offers no guidance to companies that seek to meet customers' expectations with impossible solutions.

Disruptive Innovation Is Constantly Evolving—the Relentless Pursuit

Amazon is known for making good use of time. In a 2007 conversation with Jeff Bezos (Amazon.com CEO), Thomas A. Stewart, *HBR*'s editor in chief, and Julia Kirby, a senior editor at *HBR*, Bezos remarks, "I see no reason why it should be the case, but it tends to be—is that when we plant a seed, it tends to take five to seven years before it has a meaningful impact on the economics of the company" (Kirby et al. 2007). This is about half the time of Siemens Digitalization Program. Amazon builds a business while laying the foundation for the next. "Amazon has continued to show a knack for spotting white spaces and a willingness to jump into them, even as it works to make spaces it already occupies more productive" (Kirby et al. 2007), which points to two capabilities reinforced in this book: (1) ambidextrous flexibility for companies to target growth throughout their innovation portfolios and (2) detecting disruptions across all customer expectations for companies to position.

Amazon's S team (short for "Senior team") gets together once a week for four hours and once or twice a year for two days to discuss business ideas (Kirby et al. 2007). According to Bezos, nothing in those meetings would be considered urgent, so there is time to discuss ideas. This strategic pause to afford the team tempered and measured decision-making is important. One of the challenges Bezos identified for incumbents is overcoming all of the critics, who will question new initiatives; "even if they are wild successes, they have no meaningful impact on the company's economics for years" (Kirby et al. 2007). Unfortunately, there is no foolproof way to reassure critics that disruptive innovations will be well received. Bezos captures this point well in his comment:

> [Amazon] may not know what it's going to turn [xyz] into, but at least we know that it can turn out to be big. I think you need to make sure with the things you choose that you are able to say, "If we can get this to work, it will be big." An important question to ask is, "Is it big enough to be meaningful to the company as a whole if we're very successful?" (Kirby et al. 2007).

In the same interview, Bezos talks about Amazon.com's "cultural point of view" and how it informs the business (Kirby et al. 2007). Based on Amazon's steady launch of new product offerings and tweaking its customer experience, the apparent focus for Amazon's innovation inspiration is customers. The following statements by Bezos reinforce Amazon.com's focus on customers:

- In his answer to this question: "*What are some of the things you're counting on not to change?* For our business, most of them turn out to be customer insights. Look at what's important to the customers in our consumer-facing business" (Kirby et al. 2007).
- "Another thing that we believe is pretty fundamental is that the world is getting increasingly transparent—that information perfection is on the rise. If you believe that, it becomes strategically smart to align yourself with the customer" (Kirby et al. 2007).
- "I am congenitally customer focused. And I think from that comes this passion to figure out customer-focused strategies as opposed to, say, competitor-focused strategies" (Kirby et al. 2007).
- "[A] lot of our energy and drive as a company, as a culture, comes from trying to build these customer-focused strategies.

And actually I do think they work better in fast-changing environments" (Kirby et al. 2007).

- "[I]n our environment there's so much rapid change on the Internet, in technology, that our customer-obsessed approach is very effective" (Kirby et al. 2007).

- "There's another situation, too, where I think being customer focused is better, and that's when you're a leader" (Kirby et al. 2007).

- "I'm not claiming we invented this approach—a lot of companies are customer focused—but it's very deeply ingrained in all the nooks and crannies of our culture" (Kirby et al. 2007).

For this reason, Amazon's innovations have a better chance of redefining customer expectations and leading disruption across customer types. These are all important lessons for the *Pattern of Disruptions*. From its leadership position, Amazon sets the pace and direction. Once a disruptive innovation redefines customers' expectations within a disrupter, the disruptive innovation starts the pattern over from the beginning, taking on its own path through the pattern, and leaving behind everything it disrupted. Bezos says, "We have the opportunity for Amazon not just to be a customer-centric company but to set a new standard globally for what 'customer-centric' means" (Kirby et al. 2007).

Bezos helped reinforce the meaning of staying focused on customers' expectations, which grounds the *Pattern of Disruptions*. Companies that survive and thrive through cycles of new technologies, global market expansion, and increasing competition know how to evolve by remaining observant and connected to customers. A business must work hard to develop capabilities that will deliver on and evolve with customers' expectations.

The *Pattern of Disruptions* documents a cycle of escalating customers' expectations in categories. It also evolves based on the adoption of available technologies, infrastructure, and people's tastes. The pattern helps companies identify places to look for opportunities. It does not replace the actual work. Identifying the specific expectations for products, services, business models, and markets is the work of innovators. In fact, this is where the work starts. Innovating to solve for the right problems is critical.

Christensen offered one tool he referred to as "job hunting," a mindset to garner a different perspective on a known problem or challenge (Christensen et al. 2016). Christensen shared a story from a fellow Detroiter, the same person who challenged Christensen to provide an offense to his defensive original *Theory of Disruptive Innovation*. His name is Bob Moestra. Moestra was working with a mid-size Detroit building company looking to develop homes for "downsizers." The builder struggled to sell the units. So Moestra interviewed those who bought into the building, asking "why"? The conversations pointed to "the dining room table" (Christensen et al. 2016). After having dinner in his dining room, surrounded by his own family, Moestra had a moment of clarity. Buyers were not interested in fitting in the dining room table. They wanted the memories and what it symbolized: family get-togethers, forts, birthdays, and homework. So Moestra translated the meaning behind the dining room table for downsizers. "I went in thinking we were in the business of new home construction," recalls Moestra. "But I realized we were instead in the business of moving lives" (Christensen et al. 2016). "[T]he problem lies not in the tools you're using, but what you are looking for and how you piece your observations together" (Christensen et al. 2016). Christensen does not identify a pattern of escalating customers' expectations to guide the "job hunt" or specify the disruption, but this book does that work. Having the *Pattern of Disruptions* as a rubric to guide the "hunt" is helpful.

Digital Could Be a Mass Extinction Event

Digital will only increase the speed of market shifts, expansions, and pivots, resulting in many companies falling behind—too far to catch up. Rogers highlights "five domains of strategy that digital is changing" (2016): value creation (e.g., platforms), data (e.g., connected devices), innovation tools and methods (e.g., machine learning), customers (e.g., expectations and insights), and competition (e.g., new operating models). This is an earthquake of changes for any company, and it will prove insurmountable for many. I addressed each one of these domains in this book and apply them specifically to the practice of disruptive innovation: value creation (e.g., customers' expectations and consumers' purchasing behaviors), data (e.g., digital data acquisition and connected devices), innovation tools and methods (e.g., models, frameworks, methods, and strategies), customers (e.g, loyalty-loops and customer analysis methods) and competition (e.g., maneuvering within innovation S curves). I add another layer to innovation tools and methods in the next chapter with my *Innovation Growth Maturity* framework to help companies calibrate their innovation capabilities and to determine where they have gaps.

Businesses cannot survive without new growth. The chasm between traditional business and the digital economy cannot be bridged with only assets and operating models from established businesses. There are limits to the returns on core incremental innovations, increasing productivity (automation) and process (efficiencies). Innovating only in the core will close a portion of a company's growth gap. "Traditional strategic-planning methods are useful in stretching the revenue S curve of an existing business, but they can't help companies detect how the basis for competition in a market will change" (Nunes et al. 2011). Do not manage your financial S curves alone. Manage your customers' expectations, your value creation, and your innovation S curves. Financials are lagging indicators for disruptive innovation. Therefore, every year a company does not innovate outside of its core the growth gap increases. Companies that track these growth gaps will understand where shortfalls originate (across their innovation portfolio and sales forecast). Unfortunately, the more time that passes, their customer insights diminish and their understanding of future customers' expectations is obstructed. This lost time cannot be recovered. The market will have moved on; competitors and new entrants will seize large sections of the market. Businesses trying to recover under these conditions will stall.

Thomas Siebel frames the challenge well. He builds off of works by Professor Daniel Bell, renowned author most famous for coining the term "Post-Industry Society," and Stephen Jay Gould's "new theory of evolution in *Punctuated Equilibrium.*" Siebel recognized patterns and meanings through these authors and many other conversations with industry leaders. He distills them into "evolutionary punctuations": points in time when disruptions create new energy sources (light and oxygen) and new life (species). If digital transformation is an "evolutionary punctuation" then what follows is mass disruption and constant change. Digital is a new business species. Technologies (cloud computing, big data, IoT, AI— machine learning) are the new energy sources. One needs only to read the headlines. Since 2000, 52 percent of *Fortune 500* companies have been acquired, merged, or dissolved through bankruptcy. Since the Great Recession, there has been a 40-percent turnover of the *Global Top 100* companies. When these are the chances of extinction then failure is not an option.

Key Takeaways From Chapter 5

- A key benefit of disruptive innovation and digital transformation are their abilities to create "first-mover advantage" in a variety of circumstances—just beware of being overconfident.
- Companies that master the techniques and methods in *DICE* are in the best position to play by the new digital rules for businesses enabled with digital transformation capabilities.
- Digitizing business processes and methods without a keen focus on new growth will limit a company's strategic choices and shrink its opportunities to maneuver within the innovation S curve (talent, capabilities, and competitors).
- Building digital capabilities outside of an emphasis on customers is a waste of time.
- *Part 3: It's Mastery* is complete.

PART IV

It's Control

CHAPTER 6

Hold the Line and Prepare to Advance

Digitization is impacting all aspects of our lives. As more things are digitized, they grow the digital economy. It is improbable that any business will escape the impacts of digital. However, currently the extent of digitization varies by sector (Manyika 2016). This means the digital infrastructure and capabilities across companies and countries will vary widely. These incongruences disguise the disruptive nature of digital: the scale, the scope, and the pace of change. As technologies proliferate (e.g., cloud computing and data storage, machine learning, IoT, and mobile connectivity), they will accelerate digitization and digital economies. These inconsistencies could mislead business leaders. Business leaders who do not feel the immediate pressures from customers to develop digitally enabled products, services, and business models—to create new value—might be left with the impression that digital disruption will not impact their businesses. Inconsistencies are not an indication that digital will not have an impact.

Some business leaders will understand this and continue innovating, focusing on all aspects of innovation across their portfolios: core, adjacent, and transformational. They will maintain their investments in innovation competencies with the foreknowledge that digital disrupters are not "if" but "when." They will leverage the content in this book and plan accordingly: monitoring their industries, scanning the edges of their markets through innovation ecosystems and partnerships, building digital capabilities to match current customers' expectations for value creation, tracking future disrupters in the *Pattern of Disruptions* for new customers' expectations, and planning to disrupt when the circumstances arise. These behaviors will improve a company's reaction time, and ensure the work that has been done on strategic maneuvers is ready to deploy. This is the goal: to create innovation DNA inside your business. This is the focus of this chapter. There is a military phrase that summarizes the positioning strategy I just recommended—"Hold the Line." It means to maintain your position. The phrase does not translate literally: there is no physical line and you most certainly cannot grip it in your hands. However, military service women and men understand it, as defend the territory and do not withdraw. It dates back to soldiers in lines of battle formation, and the meaning has not changed. The meaning for companies to take away is: Hold your foothold, your position, and your lead.

To some extent you can see the "hold the line" strategy being used by the company formerly known as "the world's largest retailer." In 2019, Walmart's leading competitor, Amazon, surpassed it on *Forbes'* Global 2000 list of the world's biggest public companies (Debter 2019). Doug McMillon, the CEO of Walmart, made these remarks during the National Retail Federation (NRF) Big Show, where he was being honored as The Visionary at the NRF Foundation Gala: "At some point, Walmart became big and societal expectations changed. And we missed the memo" (Danziger 2018).

Starting in 2015, Walmart began increasing its focus on digital, acquiring several large and small companies: Yihaodian (B2C e-commerce company in China), Jet.com (B2C e-commerce company in the United States), and Flipkart (e-commerce platform in India), as well as a list of retailers: Shoe.com, Moosejaw, Bonobos, Eloquii, and Bare Necessities. It also acquired grocery delivery services: Parcel (the United States) and Cornershop (in Chile and in Mexico). These digital capabilities are combined with strategic partnerships (Lord & Taylor, Rakuten, Advanced Parts, and EV_1) and technology partnerships (Microsoft's cloud computing and Google's voice assistant shopper) (Danziger 2018). Walmart put a lot in its digital 'shopping cart.'

In 2018, McMillon referred to Walmart as a "technology company" (Danziger 2018). Walmart has been utilizing its new technologies starting with its Alphabot robotic carts in a store in New Hampshire, an automated grocery cart that streamlines order processing and delivers items to Walmart employees at picking stations ready to deliver directly to customers waiting in their parked cars (Boyle 2020). "Walmart has a scaled-down version near its headquarters in Arkansas and plans to start construction of an Alphabot system this year next to its Burbank store as well as another next to a store in Mustang, Oklahoma" (Boyle 2020). This is just one of the investments Walmart is making to in-store automation to enhance "operations efficiency within its nearly 5,000 stores" (Danziger

2018). And it appears to be paying off. Walmart's online grocery business has been a star amongst its e-commerce businesses. Walmart's 2019 first-quarter earnings results showed promise. "Online grocery remains a meaningful contributor to e-commerce growth," according to Brett Biggs, Walmart's Chief Financial Officer (Garcia 2019).

Although Walmart is making inroads to "hold the line" against its main e-commerce competitor, Amazon, there is still the operating model that prevents it from earning more profits. Walmart has had to increase the number of brands it offers and the amount of inventory it carries in its fulfillment centers, and continue to stock shelves at local stores for next day, same day, and two-day in-store pickups and deliveries. This puts pressures on Walmart's profit formula of economies-of-scale, simple selections for lower prices. Now the question becomes: *How to leverage the business models of its new digital businesses to create value and to increase profitability across the enterprise?* In the next section, I outline the portfolio approach to "hold the line."

Walmart's recent shopping spree of digital investments present a communications challenge that reminds me of another military phrase from the U.S. Navy: "Nav, Conn Aye." My husband is a retired U.S. Navy Captain (U.S. Naval Academy graduate "with distinction"). I have heard my fair share of conversations that were a mix of American English and shorthand Navy. During his active duty he served on a submarine, where life and death are ever present in a submerged large metal tube equipped with nuclear warheads beneath the ocean at depths no human can survive without serious equipment and training—not to mention being responsible for the lives of over one hundred service women and men. This is why commands are direct in standard terminology understood by all through their iterative training. There is a system for verbatim repeat back to confirm orders and to ensure they are properly communicated, which minimizes confusion in times of stress (combat). For example, a Navigator ("Nav") will convey recommended ship turns. "The Conn" has responsibility for giving orders to drive the ship (typically the Officer of the Deck). "The Conn" will reply "Nav, Conn Aye." This reply means: "message received and understood." This shorthand is possible because everyone receives the same training and the same communication phasing. The meaning for companies is: Accelerate with strategic clarity in terms that everyone understands.

The direct language to communicate ("Nav, Con Aye") maneuvers between "Navigators" and the "Conn" could be a challenge for Walmart's new digital dream team: Marc Lore (Jet.com), Andy Dun (Bonobos.com), Jenny Fleiss (Rent-the-Runway cofounder and now heading up the company's Story No8 technology incubator, whose mission is to "Create the future of retails"), and Denis Incandela (Saks)," as well as Janey Whiteside (formerly with America Express), as the first customer officer focused on the customers' journey across platforms, online sites, and in-store experiences (Danziger 2018). However, if Walmart leverages the common language, I included in previous chapters, it can moboliize its teams effectively.

The Innovation Growth Maturity Framework

Throughout the book I convey the need to build capabilities across the portfolio from finding new business opportunities to transforming a sustaining business for new growth. No company can be all things, but every company should be prepared to maneuver through cycles (technologies, financial, innovation, etc.). This means having a complete understanding of the options: business models, platforms, technologies, partner networks, business and innovation ecosystems, as well as supply chain and value chain. It also means having robust systems, processes, value propositions, and profit formulas to navigate a matrix of strategic choices. In the following Table 6.1, I outline a framework of innovation competencies every organization must be aware of in order to gage their level of maturity to tackle a variety of innovation challenges. The framework should be interpreted in this way:

- The levels are building blocks.
- The ascending levels indicate maturity.
- The levels are in order for directional purposes, but they are not intended to dissuade businesses from deploying any capabilities fitting the problem.
- Although the framework stops at disruptive innovation, there will be other forms of innovation that are created, requiring new and more levels of "Innovation Growth Maturity."

Table 6.1 Innovation Growth Maturity

Growth*	Level 1: ad hoc	Level 2: incremental	Level 3: repeatable	Level 4: internalized	Level 5: optimized	Level 6: breakthrough	Level 7: disruptive
"Opportunistic": market dynamics	Reactionary	Developing line extensions and processes	Systematic approach to evaluate "strategic fit"	Projects assessed for value creation/value capture	Some movement into adjacencies. Business model innovation	Balanced portfolio/right mix: incremental, adjacencies, transformations	Joining networked ecosystems and leveraging multisided platforms to generate network effects.
"Needs": markets and customers		Primarily focused on existing customers for NPD (e.g., RFQ, proposals, quotes)	Routinely engages the market for "jobs to be done" and new ways to hire (e.g., voice of customer, observations, and experiments)	Innovation management, e.g., governance, roadmaps, project and portfolio reviews	New product and service launches and increasing experiments/rapid prototyping/learning. Identify projects with external partners	Identifying "white space"; cocreation and open innovation. New product platforms. Digital business models	New user experiences, expanding markets by tapping into nonconsumers

*Defined by the company's strategy

Mastery of the *Innovation Growth Maturity* framework relies on companies developing the right talent, systems, and organizational resources at each level. It requires companies to look at opportunities across a range of options to reveal unexplored and undefended territories (known as "white spaces" or blind spots). Jeff Bezos (Amazon.com CEO) often quotes Alan Kay: "Perspective is worth 80 IQ points." This framework should give companies foresight—*where am I, and where should I be headed?* It will increase an organization's readiness. It is directional to offer forward progress, building across all levels to allow the organization to deploy the right capabilities for innovation challenges. Larger enterprises or more mature innovative companies likely have organizational structures to manage the workload. "Large enterprises do have some advantages when launching platform businesses. They have existing value chains, powerful alliances and partnerships with other companies, pools of talent to draw upon, and vast arsenal—including loyal customer bases" (Parker et al. 2016). However, start-up founders and entrepreneurs might be doing all of the work within smaller teams. The size of the organization is less of a factor as long as the right knowledge is within the teams. The *Innovation Growth Maturity* framework should not discourage smaller enterprises. It is good to understand what innovation growth looks like.

"For decades, businesses of all stripes have wrestled with, failed to capitalize on, or passing over unique growth opportunities that don't seem to fit in with what they already do well" (Johnson 2018). The quickest way for a company to react to a disruptive innovation is to have a clear understanding of its capabilities, including where there are gaps, starting from ad hoc (reactionary) to disruptive (transformational). There is never a simple approach that works across the myriad ways a company can grow. Companies should view the *Innovation Growth Maturity* framework as options, but understand that their probability of success will depend on their talent, competitors, and capabilities. It can never be overstated that *just* knowing the *Pattern of Disruptions* does not inoculate a company.

Looking more closely at the levels you see a progression that likely follows the growth of a business from start-up/entrepreneur "small business" to incumbent "enterprise business." This framework uses "maturity" to indicate innovation capabilities (more capabilities = "mature"). It is not an indication of the quality of those capabilities, although an assumption can be made that companies meeting the milestones listed at each level would be considerably more innovative. These companies would be able to deploy the right capabilities for the challenge. In fact, flexibility and ambidextrous movements along the framework is what you want to see from a company. The focus of this book is disruptive innovation and digital transformation. Therefore, I do not expound on capabilities for Levels 1 to 5. Nevertheless, in the next section I spend time highlighting how Level 6 breakthrough capabilities help to advance companies toward Level 7 disruptive.

These are some "best practice" methods for ideation in Table 6.2 that any organization can use that are not specific to any level.

Table 6.2 Best practices for front-end idea generation

Approaches	
Venturing individual entrepreneurs	Start-ups in early stage funding (before VCs)/tech scouts/pitch events
Internal crowdsourcing idea generation	The purpose is to hire the right people to convert knowledge into money and the right external sources
Cocreation of strategic customer value creation	The "purposeful action of partnering with strategic customers, partners or employees to ideate, problem solve, improve performance, or create a new product, service or business" (Crandell 2016)
External crowdsourcing open innovation	Solicit ideas and solutions from external parties, using four basic modes of open innovation: a traditional intellectual property contract, a partnership, a contest, or a community

Growth Engine: Breakthrough to Disruption

Much of the literature on disruptive innovation focuses on two pathways: sustaining (incremental) or disruptive (transformational). However, there is an innovation growth pathway between sustaining and disruptive. The core business can be the catalyst for breakthrough innovation through a series of adjacency moves, starting with single adjacencies (sustaining innovation) and moving through to radical adjacencies (disruptive innovation). The right business resources can evaluate core products and services against a set of criteria, which I will elaborate on later, to determine their potential to grow through adjacencies to be transformational. "A company that develops a method for repeatable adjacency moves has many advantages in terms of speed and transparency, organizational efficiency, mastery of hidden detail, and reduced complexity" (Zook et al. 2003).

In 2003, *Harvard Business Review* published the results from "a five-year study of corporate growth involving 1,850 companies" conducted by Chris Zook and James Allen on growing the core through single adjacencies. The study "analyzed 181 adjacency moves," tracked single core adjacencies, and linked them back to individual company performance. "The average company succeeds only 25% of the time in launching new initiatives" (Zook et al. 2003). I ask: *With 75-percent of new initiatives failing, were some growth options missed by these companies?* The study excluded platform adjacencies with its implications on core growth and ignored R&D incremental core innovations (such as business models, resource development, and hiring). In my opinion, because the study omitted these aspects, it missed pathways to growth. Here is how I explain my thought processes: Zook and Allen's research revealed six adjacencies that I regrouped into three larger ("major") adjacency categories. They reveal pathways to growth:

- *Single adjacencies*: Core—"Company pushes out the boundaries of its core business into an adjacent space" (Zook et al. 2003).
  1. "Grow new products and services."
  2. "Address new customer segments, often by modifying a proven product or technology."
  3. "Use new distribution channels" (e.g., physical stores to e-commerce).
- *Platform adjacencies*: Adjacent—"creates groups, user communities and markets with network effects that enable users to benefit from similar or same needs by harnessing and creating large scalable technologies, products, services, and resources" (Van Alstyne et al. 2016).

4. "Expand along the value chain" (e.g., from wholesaler to direct-to-consumer) (Zook et al. 2003).

5. "Enter new geographies" (e.g., new operating models) (Zook et al. 2003).

- *Radical adjacencies*: Transformational—"is an acquisition or market move that takes the buyer or executing company into areas where its management has no, or little, current experience" (Shaughnessy 2011).

6. "Move into the 'white space' with a new business built around a strong capability" (e.g., move from physical products and services to virtual products and services) (Zook et al. 2003).

In Figure 6.1, I illustrate how the 3 major adjacency categories are interconnected—shown as concentric circles, overlapping adjacencies across the innovation portfolio (core, adjacent, transformational). This creates pathways that can be used for iterative cycles between core and transformation. Once a disruptive innovation becomes core business (like any other core product or service) it can be evaluated for a single adjacency, then evaluated for a platform adjacency, and later evaluated for a radical adjacency. These adjacencies offer the potential to expand inside a disrupter within the *Pattern of Disruptions* or to create a new market in an upcoming disrupter. "Companies that appropriately allocate resources across core, adjacent and transformational programs outperform their peers based on share price and long-term cumulative return on innovation" (Nagji et al. 2012).

Within each dimension in the *DICE* theory, there are levels and layers of decision-making. Businesses must combine their innovation competencies with their digital transformation capabilities. Although there are other frameworks for managing a core business while developing capabilities to lead transformation into new markets or businesses (Anthony et al. 2017), I determined through my analysis framework in Figure 6.1 that breakthrough adjacencies offer a company many options for transformation and maneuvers—in fact, countless maneuvers when platforms are considered. The possibilities increase with platforms (multisided and networked in an ecosystem).

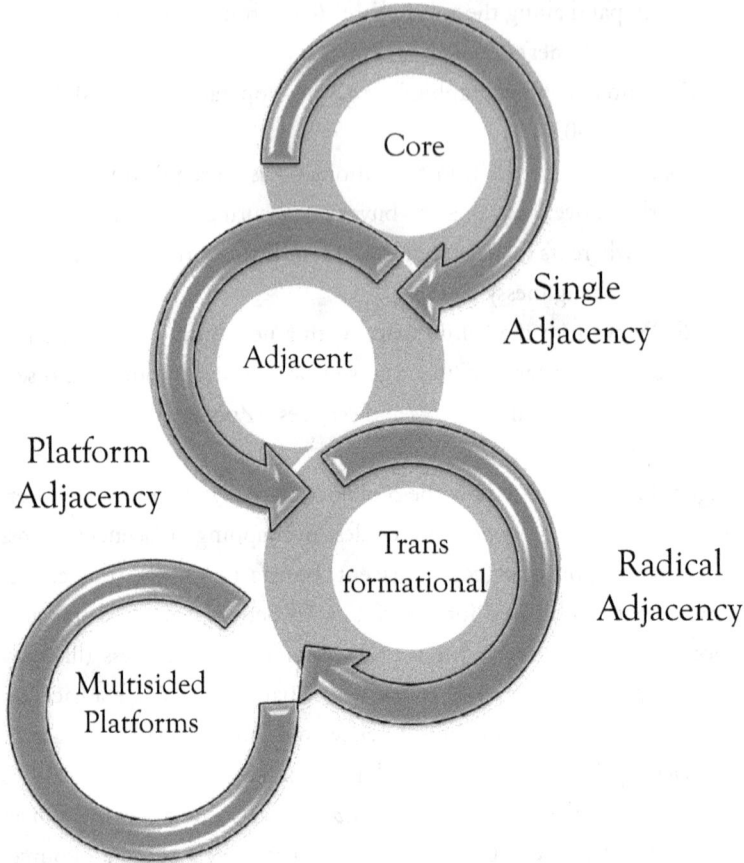

Figure 6.1 Breakthrough adjacencies

Multisided Platforms (MSP)

No network effects are generated in single-sided platforms. "Network effects" only exist in MSPs, when value is increased—beyond the transactional face value of products or services—with every increase in users there is an increase in providers. MSPs accelerate business models (network effects) and profit formulas (exponential value creation). The number of sides of a MSP depend on the number of partners needed to create value for end-customers. The number of sides and their identities must be relevant (Hagui 2013). When an incumbent "pipeline" business—designed for "economies-of-scale" (supply side)—becomes a platform business it is adding "economies-of-scope" (demand side) to its operating model, which changes its profit formula. It becomes a continuous loop that enables a company to better align its supply and demand with its products, services, business models, and operations to its value creation and value propositions. MSPs become extremely valuable in Networked Ecosystems. (I cover Networked Ecosystems in the next chapter).

Continuing from Figure 6.1, here are the conditions for a Radical Adjacency developing into a MSP (Van Alstyne et al. 2016; Hagui et al. 2017):

- The company has a large customer base and has a strong brand—yet it leaves a diverse set of customers with unmet needs.
- Customers have frequent interactions (both inside and outside of the company's existing platform adjacency).
- Two sets of products/services—serving different customers.
- Some overlap between the company's customers and its external partners' customers.
- Products/services can benefit from network affects.

Following this assessment, a company must decide if it should build a MSP or if it should join (supply into) a MSP to expand its own offerings, as well as build brand loyalty and gain access to more data and insights on customers. Companies must consider the possibility that they could build or join a "lopsided" MSP—favoring one partner's capabilities over another. If a company finds itself in a lopsided MSP then here are a few pieces of advice: acknowledge the deficit by managing the expectations of your customers; monitor any bypass methods that move interactions from inside the MSP to the outside (favoring one partner); and watch for confusing offerings that share products/services across partners without a clear assignment of value created.

Here are the conditions for joining or building an MSP:

1. "Build it" if the company has more expertise (subject matter skills and talents) but not more consistent quality delivery methods.
2. "Join in" (or supply into) if the company has more consistent quality delivery methods but not more expertise (subject matter skills and talents).

In 2017, of the 10 most valued companies in the world by market cap (Kiesnoski 2017), 5 derived much of their worth from their MSPs that facilitated interactions or transactions between parties: Microsoft (Azure), Facebook, Amazon.com, Alphabet (Google), and Apple (iOS). Many MSPs are more valuable than companies in the same industries that provide only products or services (Hagui et al. 2017). However, platforms are not immune to being disrupted by new technologies. To ensure an MSP remains relevant: think how it can make these elements interactive and interchangeable to "produce faster, scale faster, work faster" (Siebel 2019). Think about how to use the MSP's data to move a business forward. Data can power AI (machine learning) operating models, build social networks matchmaking, and foster network effects.

Words of caution from Marco Iansiti and Karim R. Lakhani in their article, "Competing in the Age of AI":

"it can take quite a while for AI-driven operating models to generate economic value, anywhere close to the value that traditional operating models generate at scale" (Iansiti et al. 2020). In order to generate value from "network effects" it takes reaching a critical mass for the application or service, "and most newly applied algorithms suffer from a 'cold start' before acquiring adequate data" (Iansiti et al. 2020). "The AI-driven search, recommendation, and matchmaking on Amazon, Google, Waymo/Lyft/Uber are derived from data that is repeatedly validated against search results, purchases, rides" (Iansiti et al. 2020).

Warnings to Incumbents

A word of caution for incumbents considering postponing or underfunding digital transformation capabilities, following are 3 scenarios that demonstrate how digital through disruptive innovation changed entire industries:

1. A company creates products and services. It ignores digital and business model innovation. It focuses on optimizing its business for operating efficiencies: incremental performance improvements and process innovations. It maxes out on growth from these levers.

A business model innovator, such as Amazon, comes along and builds digital capabilities that create, deliver, and capture new value, leveraging the nondigital products and services that the incumbent optimized. The incumbent often does not see the business model innovator coming, as it is not usually a key player in the incumbent's industry. Unfortunately, by the time the incumbent has reframed this new threat and starts to build technology enabled products, services, and business models it is already losing ground and a stall is imminent.

2. A company creates a digital product, such as Apple's iPod, but in order to create more value it needs a service. The service it needs is not optimized for digital. The music industry was distracted by multiple digital threats from compact disks and MP3 players. At the time, Apple was a computer company. Yet, it disrupted media players (Apple's iPod) and the music industry (Apple's iTunes). It entered the market where it had no prior experience (the definition of radical adjacency).

   It would be easy to think that the iPod and iTunes combination was a natural fit for Apple, that it was a low-risk extension of the company's core expertise in hardware and software system integrations. But the transformation actually represented business model reinvention, a real white-space move. Apple had been a computer maker. It had limited experience with the world of music and media and virtually no identity in the public's mind as a provider of entertainment technology (Johnson, 2018).

3. A digital native company develops a digital gaming product—enabled by a technology within a MSP. In 2001, Microsoft sought to enter the video game industry with its Xbox console and continue partnering with the producer of videogames (Hagui 2013). During this time, the videogame's relationship (1:1) was between the console and the player's handset. The console dictated the format, the type of handset, the videogames, the loading speeds, the graphics quality, and the sound volume. Microsoft developed a three-sided platform for the Xbox: videogame producers, console manufacturers, and

handset ancillary manufacturers (adapters for multi handsets, speakers, etc.). Cloud computing shifted the field. Consider the impact of multisided platforms enabled by cloud computing on the video gaming console market. A Forbes article, "There Is No Console War Because Xbox Moved On and Left PlayStation Behind," quotes Microsoft's Phil Spencer, head of Xbox: "I don't want to be in a fight over format wars with those guys [Nintendo and Sony] while Amazon and Google are focusing on how to get gaming to 7 billion people around the world. Ultimately that's the goal" (Murnane 2020). In essence, Microsoft declared it was no longer competing for the console market or "format wars" because it already won against Sony and Nintendo and had moved on to competing against Google and Amazon in the multiplayer (1:X) cloud videogaming market.

Previously, I mentioned the year 2007, was a digital inflection point. Figure 6.1 is a strategic inflection point. It changes the threat framing—by changing the market entry point. Digital natives are not exclusively threatening incumbent core businesses through low-end market entry points they are attacking a version of the business in the digital future. They use digital, technology, infrastructure and data from billons of products and services to envision the path of a business, creating value to meet future customers' expectations. When they are successful with their attacks they alter an incumbent business' strategic choices in the future. They disrupt at radical (transformation), building adjacencies, and then creating multisided platform business models. These digital natives move the threat away from the incumbent's core. "They [digital natives and digitally-enabled new entrants] pull industries in new digital directions while gaining a huge head start in reaping the benefits from the new models they are creating. This forces incumbents into a race to catch up" (Bughin et al. 2017). It has been stated many times before, but I will repeat it again: digital transformation changes the rules of business, and adaptation through disruptive innovation is a matter of survival.

Iterative Growth Engine for Breakthrough Innovation

This book offers an iterative growth engine that can help companies, using breakthrough adjacencies in Figure 6.1. As follows I outline it in three (3) phases. I used a "phenomenon-driven approach" to focus on capturing, documenting, and conceptualizing the phenomena I observed. I leveraged a white paper published in 2015 by ReD Associates, "Growing Beyond the Core—How a Phenomenon-Driven Approach Can Help You Build Adjacency Platform Growth" (Vangsgaard et al. 2015) to systematize my approach. "In almost any industry you care to examine, the most dramatic stories of growth and success were launched from a platform of disruptive innovation" (Christensen et al. 2003).

Phase A: When applied to breakthrough adjacencies observe three criteria to identify the strongest core single product/service to develop into a core "single adjacency":

1. An identifiable pocket of growth—a big potential market.
2. An unresolved customer/consumer aspiration or need—there is a gap between what customers need and what the company currently offers.
3. An indication of commercial viability—there is money to be made.

For example:

> Nike begins by establishing a leading position in athletic shoes in the target market. Next, Nike launches a clothing line endorsed by the sport's top athletes—like Tiger Woods, whose $100 million deal in 1996 gave Nike the visibility it needed to get traction in golf apparel and accessories. Expanding into new categories allows the company to forge new distribution channels and lock in suppliers. Then it starts to feed higher-margin equipment into the market—irons first, in the case of golf clubs, and subsequently drivers. In the final step, Nike moves beyond the U.S. market to global distribution. (Zook et al. 2003)

Note: Consider shifts in customers' expectations in the core over time when initiating a "first-mover advantage" into a single adjacency.

Phase B: Perform these four analysis steps to develop the strongest single adjacent into a "platform adjacency":

1. Focus exclusively on the strongest single adjacent—avoid carrying over legacy features that are no longer strengths.
2. Follow an evidenced-based problem-solving process.
3. Harvest data from a wide variety of complementary methods—using a triangulation data approach and observed data over time in a longitudinal approach.
4. Apply a structured framework that is repeatable—make it concrete and systematic.

Phase C: Transformational products and services can be developed into a Radical Adjacency when increased value can be created by external partners. This requires building ecosystems with partners (suppliers and customers) to develop multisided platforms.

Business Model Innovation for Breakthrough Innovation

The business model is how resources and processes create, deliver, and capture value for customers through products and services while sustaining value (profit) for the business and its key stakeholders. The operating model is the delivery method for value created from the business model. When the products and services that underpin a business model are being disrupted the argument to improve operating efficiency does not work. It might temporarily help the bottom-line, such as through process innovations. However, it does not address changing customers' expectations, which are likely to increase and to solidify while a company optimizes its cost savings and efficiency measures. As customers' needs evolve, the business model must recalibrate to meet those new demands. I gave a detailed example of this with the ICE passenger vehicle and rideshare business model innovations.

There is a way to discover new customer expectations for a product and service through the operating model and not wait for the product and service innovators to reach those conclusions. Earlier in the book, I explained the value of "jobs mapping" contrasted against "process mapping" to reveal areas to create outcome-driven innovation. This methodology also can be used to inform which areas in the operating model can be eliminated, optimized, and/or revised to innovate the business model. This is where new technologies offer new or expanded capabilities. Although new technologies are enablers, they are not the solution (Johnson 2018). The right business model creates the environment for a technology to be an advantage, as well as an instrument for exploration into new growth areas. This combined with customer insights is powerful. "Executives can begin by systemically examining each core element of their business model, which typically comprises customer relationships, key activities, strategic resources, and the economic models' cost structure and revenue streams" (de Jong et al. 2015). The common denominator that readies these elements for transformation is digitization. It changes the rules, "which upends customer interactions, business activities, the deployment of resources, and economic models" (de Jong et al. 2015). This work becomes more difficult if a company has moved away from scanning and monitoring for shifts in customer expectations, and it worsens if a company's growth is already stalled. The *Pattern of Disruptions* lays out the disrupter breadcrumbs for companies to follow to avoid missteps. Nevertheless, the pattern is a recommendation. If a company decides to remain in a particular market position, despite indications that the market is reaching saturation, that is, additional innovations will not yield a higher price, then leaders should reread the conditions for jumping and climbing innovation S curves. A challenge to the business model can yield growth opportunities. This is where *DICE* provides methodologies to reveal new customers' expectations and reimage the business model for new value creation.

Table 6.3 helps companies on the outside of the product, service, or business model arrive at customers' expectations from their perspectives: (1) investigate inefficiencies in the business model's operating model to deliver more value, (2) identify how that value will be created and captured in a business model, and (3) target the areas where the value created matches customers' expectations. Businesses can leverage the insights, approaches, and frameworks in this book or other best practices in their arsenals. The following Table 6.3 outlines some combinations of innovation focuses, business models, growth opportunities, and methodologies:

Table 6.3 New growth opportunity business model matrix

New customers	PLATFORM INNOVATION [business model] "Platform or MSP adjacencies" [growth opportunities] Unrealized expectations met through external partnerships [methodology] Breakthrough adjacencies	DISRUPTIVE INNOVATION [business model] "Radical adjacencies" [growth opportunities] Nonconsumers [methodology] Observations through engaging experiences/environments
Existing customers	INCREMENTAL INNOVATION [business model] "Single adjacencies" [growth opportunities] Digital channels (brands) [methodology] Customer loyalty loops	INCREMENTAL INNOVATION [business model] "White space – new business model" [growth opportunities] New user experiences Shared consumption [methodology] Environments (start joining)
	Latent customers	Future customers (non-consumers)

A System That Can Learn

In one of my favorite books on machine learning, *Machine Platform Crowd*, Andrew McAfee and Brynjolfsson describe the human challenges of playing the game Go ("a pure strategy game—no luck involved [game theorist would call Go "deterministic perfect information game"]—developed a least 2,500 years ago in China" (McAfee et al. 2017)). I have never played Go, but I am intrigued to take on the challenge. Nevertheless, a human team at Google's DeepMind, "a London-based company specializing in machine learning," built a program, AlphaGo, a Go-playing application that ultimately beat the best human Go player on the planet, Lee Sedol (Seoul, South Korea), in a five-game match (McAfee et al. 2017). The AlphaGo team did not try to repeat the winning strategies of past players. "Instead, they created a system that could learn them on its own" (McAfee et al. 2017). "A system that could learn" is my hope for this book, a disruptive innovation system for digital transformation. Understanding the pathways between the core and transformation, the cycles of adjacencies into platforms, and *Innovation Growth Maturity Framework* will help companies build an iterative engine for new disruptive innovation. A company can leverage the systematic and repeatable elements to build an iterative engine and to build confidence within teams to act with strategic clarity. This translates into "learning-curve benefits, increased speed, and lower complexity" (Zook et al. 2003).

Unfortunately, there are organizational considerations that constrain companies from pursuing growth through breakthrough adjacency methods. Zook and Allen (2003) cautioned in their research about some particularly damaging behaviors in any organization looking to lead in disruptive innovation.

1. "These executives also wouldn't make a move unless they had a good shot at being one of the top three players in a new space" (Zook et al. 2003).
   - Time is not on our side, and distributed authority to make business decisions will be required. The ability to "move" in minor ways is necessary for market expansions through upmarket plays, for example, performance, quality, and functionalities.
2. "And although they constantly scanned for opportunities, they pursued only one at a time" (Zook et al. 2003).
   - A talented ambidextrous organization that is capable of maneuvering through the disrupters and between them will prevent a company from stalling and allow it to manage flexible strategies for jumping and climbing.
3. Companies should factor into adjacency moves: the pace of change in customers' expectations, the speed of technology adoption, and the changes to the operating model.
4. Companies should also examine how they budget resources in ways that isolate the R&D organization behind activities, creating divisions-of-labor:
   - Core sustaining activities—focus on incremental improvements in existing innovations, processes, features, and so on.
   - Adjacent step-out activities—focus on moving into nearby markets and technologies.
   - Transformational disruptive activities—focus on finding/creating new markets and/or finding/creating new technologies.

Key Takeaways From Chapter 6

- Accelerate with strategic clarity in terms that everyone understands.
- To reach disruptive innovation in the *Innovation Growth Maturity Framework* start by acknowledging where a company currently resides along the spectrum of capabilities.
- Best practices can be leveraged across an organization for all types of innovation.
- Breakthrough adjacencies unlock pathways to new growth in between core innovations and transformational innovations.
- Digital unlocks new business model innovations.

CHAPTER 7

Open Innovation and Networked Ecosystems

Throughout the previous chapters, I sounded alarms for new growth by identifying opportunities for market expansion and market creation through the *Pattern of Disruptions*, revealing strategic business maneuvers, using the dimensions in the *DICE Theory*, reinventing interactions with customers, building digital and innovation competencies, and iteratively systematizing growth throughout the portfolio. It is important to articulate and to advise companies on the need for these organizational competencies for disruptive innovation and digital transformation in the 21st-century.

However, there are other resources available to companies to grow by leveraging external resources. "Open innovation stresses the importance of the external knowledge activity of a company during the innovation process" (Park 2017). Open innovation offers companies ways to rebalance their capabilities, factoring in internal talent, and identifying resources with external expertise and skills. Open innovation has been a tool in the growth arsenal for centuries. Inventors were founders during the Industrial Revolution: 1760 to 1830. They tapped into open innovation to accelerate manufacturing equipment, designs, tools, processes, new technologies, advance engineering methods, and scientific explorations. History has kept a record of inventors and designers collaborating, sharing, and ideating.

In 19th-century Britain, those include blast furnace technology for making iron, the high pressure steam engine in the Cornish mining district, textile equipment, the development of coal burning houses in London, and advances in civil engineering. During the same period in the United States, innovators shared designs and other knowledge in the cotton textile industry, in the high-pressure steam engine for western steamboats, in paper-making, in the Bessemer process for making steel, and among mechanics generally. In addition, American and British farmers swapped ideas frequently, including methods of crop rotation and extensive biological innovation in wheat, cotton, tobacco, alfalfa, corn, and livestock. (Bessen 2014)

Undoubtedly, with the speed of digital the need for open innovation in Industry 4.0 IoT is drastically different. Unlike during the first Industrial Revolution, open innovation now comprises "different applications like joint R & D, technology transfer, licensing, open source software, and mass sources (crowdsource) that provide outbound and inbound flow of information" (Ozkan 2015). They can be highly effective when exposing a problem to a large community with a broad range of skills. Therefore, open innovation can identify expert capabilities (e.g., talent, skills, equipment, methods) and generate ideas around opportunity areas, as well as identify emerging technologies and innovation tools, methods, and applications. "Opportunity areas" are identified as gaps between what customers or buyers expect and what a company currently offers as a solution. Open innovation can uncover new solution spaces and new problem spaces for digital, technology, and IoT connectivity.

It is also an excellent starting point for collaboration. Digital expands the opportunities for collaboration: big data, virtual products and services, platform partnerships, and a host of future opportunities. Each area has its own set of unique challenges, for example, data (volume, velocity, and variety), system and network compatibility across suppliers, as well as predictive results from AI machine learning algorithms, experiments, tests, and simulations. "Fewer than 30% of a company's technology vendors are actively involved in their digital transformations" (*Forbes* 2019). Finding partners capable of receiving open and networked data to reconfigure products and features can be a challenge. This also impacts leveraging digitally enabled platforms. As the volume of data increases due to mass-customizations and hyper-personalization, digital transformation becomes more important in partner engagements. Organizations could be overwhelmed with the volume of changes from customers, competitors, and technologies. Organizations could find themselves insufficiently matched for the pace and find they need help to simultaneously play defense and offense. A business that has mastered the inside organization can influence and direct additional resources from the outside to distribute talent and resources across a portfolio of projects with defined scopes of work, to access specialists across time zones and languages and to be agile (learn, pivot, fail fast). This is one of the values of open innovation.

There are several large crowdsourcing open innovation platforms, some managed by companies, universities, government labs, and others by third parties. In Table 7.1, I included a nonexhaustive list of open innovation platforms as references. There are three primary approaches to collaboration on open innovation platforms: commercial agenda, community agenda, and a hybrid agenda (both commercial and community). I ask that you conduct your own research into these resources and determine how best to utilize them. In addition to these open innovation platforms, there are contests (e.g., government labs: NIST and NASA), idea contest aggregators (e.g., IdeaConnection by Planbox), expert communities (e.g., NineSigma and InnoCentive), and intellectual property search engines (e.g., Yet2.com). There are also literature exploration tools powered by artificial intelligence (AI) (e.g., Iris.ai.), advanced technology scouts and analysts (e.g., Lux Research and Mary Meeker's Internet Trend reports), as well as start-up incubators and matchmakers (e.g., MaRS Discovery District and Plug-and-Play).

Table 7.1 Open innovation platforms

Open innovation platforms	Commercial agenda "Brokering expertise" building internal capabilities targeting specific idea types and opportunities, that is, promising ideas with some degree of success already, within the innovation capabilities of a company (or in partnership with other companies)	Community agenda "Connecting with lead users" to target early trends and to capture ideas. They are not required to conform to a commercial product/ service offering. Community users may ask for buy-in (via votes) from the community to rank ideas	Hybrid agenda Mix between commercial and community agendas
LEGO Ideas			X
Fab Labs		X	
Threadless Fashion Innovation		X	
MIT Media Lab	X		
Microsoft .NET Gadgeteer	X		X
connect + develop P&G internal open innovation tool	X		
Chaordix	X		
BrightIdea	X		
100% Open	X		
Spigit	X		
Nosco			X
idClic is Orange's internal open innovation tool	X		
Qmarkets			X
YourEncore		X	
Other design labs (e.g., Hyve, Hype)	X		

Collaboration Frameworks

Developing the environment for collaboration to support open innovation activities is a critical part of the process of importing resources and capabilities. Collaborating within these platforms requires an organization to understand the pitfalls and the benefits that could lead to mixed results. "Innovating with external partners doesn't always give companies a competitive advantage. It needs to be balanced with internal efforts" (Thomas et al. 2020). Proctor & Gamble (P&G) wanted to guarantee external resources were being leveraged to accelerate innovations. So it promoted an internal message "Look to connect and develop before you research and develop" (Cloyd et al. 2015) for its "connect & develop" platform. Consequently, I offer three sample grids for companies to matrix together their open innovation collaboration resources to build out capabilities from the outside in and to align needed resources with the various phases of innovation projects (Figure 7.1).

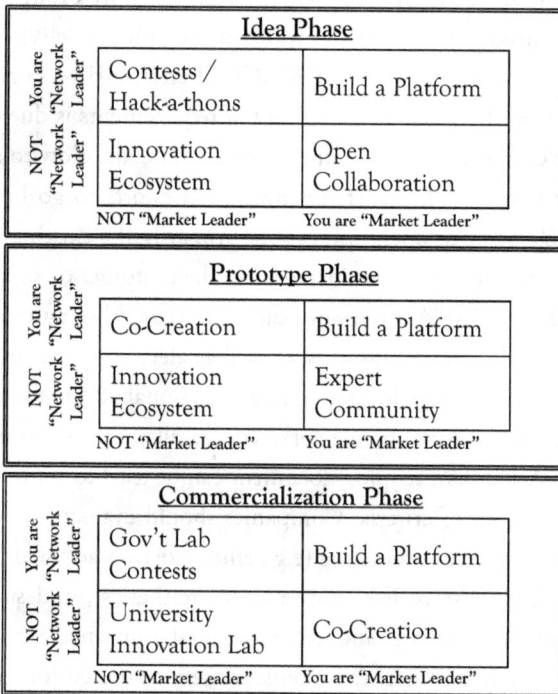

Figure 7.1 Open Innovation Collaborations Framework by Innovation Project Phase

Note: On August 21, 2020, I received a certification from MIT Sloan Corporate Innovation: Strategies for Leveraging Ecosystems. I highly recommend taking this course. It provided me with some unique insights that I leveraged in Figure 7.1. The most impactful insight for me was the MIT framework of 5-Key Stakeholders for innovation ecosystems: Risk Capital, Universities, Government, Entrepreneurs, and Corporations. Innovation ecosystems require colocation of the key stakeholders. Figure 7.1 does not include these additional elements.

Collaboration needs a framework to level set goals, to articulate needs, and to document expectations in partnership discussions, as well as to manage resources. It is a best practice way to work collaboratively and to avoid expending large amounts of effort and resources before reaching clarity on the desired outcomes. *What does success look like?* Clearly defining the expected outcomes and the measurements to be used that will satisfy all parties is important at the outset. Gil Cloyd, former Chief Technology Officer Proctor & Gamble (P&G), noted about its open innovation collaborations: "almost everything we brought in from the outside needed some modifications to be able to deliver the consumer performance that we wanted" (Cloyd et al. 2015). For instance, testing iterative designs across a battery of requirements is due diligence for a larger company, but can appear bureaucratic and slow to an entrepreneur or start-up. "In order for innovation efforts to go beyond the company to transit to open innovation, primarily the existing processes or applications should be considered from the customer or supplier outlooks" (Ozkan 2015). A framework can help to establish agreements, set parameters, and manage resources, as well as alert everyone to key decision gates. It offers more focus to guide intentional efforts for all parties to manage expectations. Frameworks ensure all projects are developed holistically. A standard scoping document can be used to vet innovations using the same set of criteria. Companies should evaluate all aspects of an innovation, such as processing (e.g., eliminate transactional frictions), experience (e.g., ease of use, convenience, aesthetics), and sustainability (e.g., reuse, materials, and environmental impacts). Scanning the entire "environment" where the product or service is used (or connected) can seem ancillary to the primary innovation—but they add value for customers.

Collaborations help to accelerate adjacency moves. "Some of the fastest-moving and elusive business opportunities for companies are adjacencies, which arise near to existing core areas of focus" (Idelchik et al. 2015). Perhaps a partner has complementary capabilities (marketplace or network) where the company has deficits, which can reduce uncertainty or reveal blind spots. This was the case for GE's Open Collaboration Model. "Open collaboration has become a strong platform for growth in adjacencies at GE, and the company has applied lessons learned from the experience of working with outside partners to transform the way innovation is done internally" (Idelchik et al. 2015). A balanced portfolio requires investments in innovations targeting adjacencies, as well as core and new business.

There are excellent examples of lessons learned by large companies from their open collaboration programs. GE learned a valuable lesson on "setting up transparent nondisclosure processes and guidelines to govern every step of the relationship has been important in reinforcing mutual trust, which is key to any collaboration" (Idelchik et al. 2015). P&G faced the challenge of internal researchers feeling threatened or devalued by the pursuit of outside technologists (Cloyd et al. 2015). As long as everyone is clear about the objectives of the collaboration this should not be a factor. P&G's "connect & develop" platform helps to define the goals and to manage expectations. "For connect and develop to work, we realized, it was crucial to know exactly what we were looking for, or 'where to play'" (Huston et al. 2006). P&G reframed their agreements with suppliers to allow for increased collaboration, for instance 'master collaboration agreements' that flowed across the business units and enabled people to engage external partners and move quickly toward final deal structures (Cloyd et al. 2015), such as reviewing intellectual patent applications, a traditionally slow process.

Another lesson that may be counterintuitive—considering most companies want to innovate quickly—is to reach beyond the established supply base. Known suppliers understand the company's processes and requirements. This knowledge can reduce the "learning-curve," but it can also limit the creative ideas and concepts brought forward. It is possible suppliers would filter out ideas and concepts not "fitting" the profile of the company. I found when the focus is on an opportunity space with a defined outcome, involving a company's known customer or supplier, cocreation is a better approach to open innovation for disruptive innovations. Cocreation agreements are exploratory. They investigate potential ways to grow—not apparent to either party. I provide a *Partnership Collaboration Framework* in Figure 7.2. to facilitate structuring the beginnings of a collaborative relationship. This is different than joint development agreements, which are defined for a specific project or application with a standard statement of work, milestones, and deliverables.

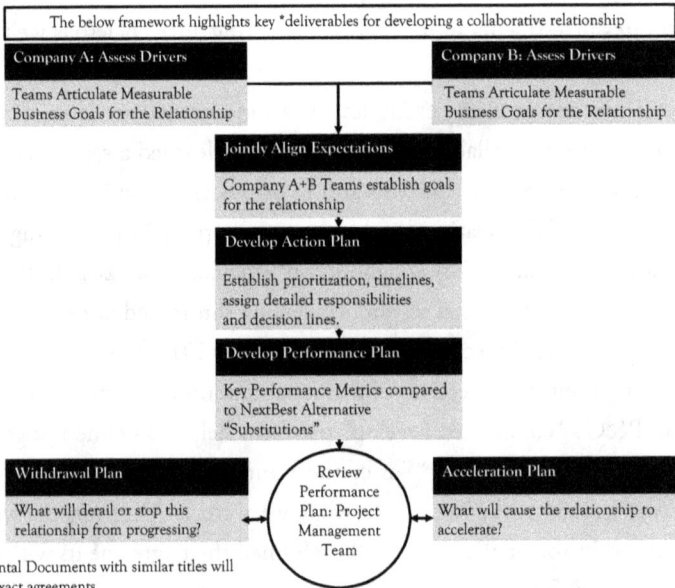

Diagram inspired by an illustration in *Building High Performance Business Relationships* by Douglas M. Lambert, A. Michael Knemeyer, and John T. Gardner4 (Supply Chain Management Institute: Sarasota, Florida, 2010, p.79)

Figure 7.2 Partnership Collaboration Framework

Cocreation can be successful in a variety of collaborative relationships:

- Cocreation with strategic suppliers is "purposeful cooperation over time, the identification and implementation of joint initiatives, and the sharing of financial gains" (Lambert et al. 2015). Having a relationship with and understanding the capabilities of the partner help to mitigate confusion and to lessen uncertainty.

- Cocreation can be a "purposeful action of partnering with strategic customers, partners or employees to ideate, problem solve, improve performance, or create a new product, service or business" (Crandell 2016). In a new relationship, where the advantages of knowing the partner are not present, I use positioning maps to visualize how partners' capabilities align with the company's capabilities. To demonstrate how a company could use a positioning map to evaluate the capabilities of potential external partners compared to its own capabilities, I created a fictional example to illustrate in the following grid (Figure 7.3). I used insights from *Platform Revolution* (Parker et al. 2016) and *LA Times* article, "J. Crew Gets Active with New Balance" (Moin 2016) to put myself in the room when J. Crew's athleisure-fitness line was selecting the best partner. In this example, I had the outcome of the decision. New Balance was the partner selected. So I considered what other partners J. Crew could have considered and plotted them on a grid (Figure 7.3).

- It is common for the fashion and electronics industries to partner in a go-to-market strategy. So I considered top brands with more network than J. Crew in the fitness electronics category (Apple watch, Garmin, and Fitbit);

- I considered fashion aggregators, stylists with more access to top brands, through distribution with more marketplace than J. Crew (Stitch Fix and Nordstrom's Trunk Club);

- I considered top brands in stylish fitness shoes with more network and more marketplace than J. Crew. I eliminated Nike, Puma, Under Armor, and Adidas because each has strong apparels brands, leaving Sketcher and New Balance.

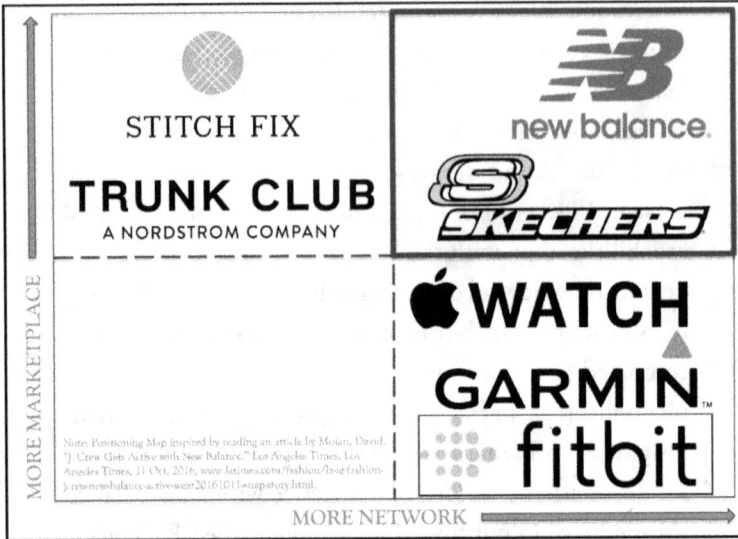

Figure 7.3 External partnership positioning map (fictional: J. Crew's decision to choose New Balance for Athleisure)

Selecting a partner with complementary capabilities is a first step; then the discussions must evolve to processes (e.g. eliminating transactional friction across operations), logistics handling (e.g. shipping/returns to the customer), new product development (e.g. cocreation and collaboration), ownership of brand promotion and pricing decisions, as well as connecting interfaces (websites/apps) to platforms, and access to data. "The innovators who hope to create the great new platforms of the future need to focus on the core interactions in the marketplace they hope to conquer, and analyze the barriers that limit them" (Parker et al. 2016). This is the aim of the grid I created: to encourage debate and to build consensus on the direction.

Revisiting Assumptions

Open innovation and collaboration are tools and methods teams can use to manage uncertainty and to mitigate risk. Whether the move is into an adjacency or into a completely new market and application, where the company's management team has no experience, getting comfortable with being uncomfortable is the new business normal. It will require an organization to revisit assumptions that may be holding them back from embracing the potential of open innovation.

One such assumption is a speculation that companies only gravitate toward open innovation when new technological capabilities are needed (Ozkan 2015). It is a clear benefit as Cloyd P&G explained, "If innovation is idea-led and technology-enabled, we really don't care where the technology comes from as long as it can drive wining innovation." However, there are other capabilities open innovation offers (Cloyd et al. 2015). The open innovation approach should always match the situation. Companies with emerging technologies can use open innovation to scan possible challenges fitting its technology's capabilities (solve or enable).

Every company has stories from its past about missteps or missed opportunities. Bezos echoes this in his interview with *HBR*:

> A lot of our strategy comes from having very deep points of view about things like this, believing that they are going to be stable over time, and making sure our activities line up with them. Of course there could also come a day when one of those things turns out to be wrong. So it's important to have some kind of mechanism to figure out if you're wrong about a deeply held precept. (Kirby et al. 2007)

Hearsay is another source of assumptions. The headlines are filled with venture capitalists investing millions into start-up companies only for those companies to burn through capital without ever becoming profitable. Large corporations prefer a more balanced approach to growth over a growth-at-all-costs approach. This is an area where *Pattern of Disruptions* can be of particular benefit to business leaders. It can help management pitch the value of a disruptive innovation, using transparent language—specific to major categories of customers' expectations—and offer examples from products, services, and business models, where the pattern provides deep insights into maneuvers. These examples can be amplified—from the production line worker to the C-suite executive—to create opportunities that are relatable using these methods (Dyer et al. 2009):

- Comparing: Finding the right analogy to convince supporters your idea will succeed.
- Materializing: Making an abstract concept tangible, visible, and real.
- Storytelling: Crafting a narrative that gives listeners a reason to believe.
- Signaling: Connecting to other credible groups that confer legitimacy on your idea.
- Applying social pressure: Creating a sense of scarcity (the feeling that people need to act now or they'll miss out).
- Committing: Convincing others through a visible, personal, or irreversible action.

Networked Innovation Ecosystems

Although this is the end of this book, it is far from the end of the journey. I dedicated the majority of the examples of disruptive innovation and digital transformation to the first 5-disrupters in the *Pattern of Disruptions*: "accessible", "dependable", "reliable", "usable", and "delightful." So I conclude with "meaningfulness." It is the last disrupter I can envision from my current perspective. It targets megatrends (e.g., climate change, sustainability, urbanization, aging) and disparities and inequalities. The "meaningfulness" disrupter will demand a mastery of disruptive innovation and digital transformation while orchestrating ecosystems and resources to tackle "big-thinking" planet-scale challenges. This is the next frontier of disruptive innovation and digital transformation. It will require developing and networking innovation ecosystems in order to keep pace with digitization, new technologies, and new ways to connect partners. The *Pattern of Disruptions* can help companies track customers' expectations and identify where there are networking opportunities to deliver increased value—across *DICE* theory dimensions and across a variety of operating models: economies-of-scope (variety), economies-of-scale (volume), and hyper-personalization.

However, there are questions. *How to connect innovation ecosystems? Must companies consider their position(s) within the value network? And, how does a company decide which innovation ecosystems can help deliver increased networked value?* Inspiration for answers to the first question, we can learn a lot from the model that gave the world the "Internet"—a network of networked ecosystems: common language "protocols," expert communication networks (NSF, Defense, etc.), domestic and international "backbones," and providers to disperse packets of information in the most efficient ways. A starting point to answer the last two questions, I looked to the *Pattern of Disruptions*, which maintains a keen focus on tapping into and meeting customers' expectations. In an article by Elizabeth J. Altman and Frank Nagle, in *MIT Sloan Management Review*, "Accelerating Innovation through a Network of Ecosystems: What Companies Can Learn from One of the World's Largest Networks of Accelerator Labs" (2020), I found more answers: innovators working collaboratively across innovation ecosystems and how they are networked. The article's focus is the United Nations Development Programme (UNDP), "an organization of 17,000 employees spanning 170 countries, focuses on solving the world's most complex problems—ending poverty, ensuring healthy lives and wellbeing, providing affordable and clean energy, reducing inequalities, and more—through local, regional, and global initiatives" (Altman et al. 2020). The UNDP was accelerating innovations through networked ecosystems (Altman et al. 2020). Basic wellness, utilities ("affordable and clean energy"), a living wage, and fairness ("reducing inequalities") are customers' expectations that are clearly in the wheelhouse for disruptive innovation and digital transformation. However, on a global scale the ambition surpasses the capabilities of any one organization's capabilities. This requires a network of innovators, a networked innovation ecosystem. UNDP is "creating a large network of ecosystems that revolve around its labs, and building connections with local partners while also helping the labs coordinate with one another" (Altman et al. 2020). This exposes its entire network of labs to the outside world.

What can businesses learn from UNDP to accelerate collaboration in a network of innovation ecosystems? First, there were some basic organizational lessons UNDP learned (Altman et al. 2020): "build on existing organizational priorities"; "close to power centers in their organizations"; consult "experts inside the organization"; and "integration across cities, countries, and regions," thus "reaping the benefits of scale and scope." Geography separated the original innovation lab teams, leaving them in isolation to solve challenges. This had one benefit: being outside of the organization free to experiment without the burden of bureaucracy. This often meant leaving out the larger organization of internal experts when consulting with external experts; "innovators ignored it, fearing that internal feedback would stall them" (Altman et al. 2020). Teams avoided the "not-invented-here" syndrome, which typically describes an internal organization's response to external concepts, ideas, and methodologies. Therefore, they did not get the attention or acknowledgement they needed to create much needed visibility. Little visibility is not good for innovation. "They weren't part of a larger network that could support sharing, cocreation, and learning" (Altman et al. 2020). UNDP had pockets of innovations and successes happening within local teams, but they were not cascaded beyond the scope of the challenge into other applications, that is, "projects were seen as one-off or ad hoc," and to other teams, that is, "they didn't change the way UNDP worked" (Altman et al. 2020).

Second, there were some basic scale lessons learned. From 2018 to 2019, UNDP recognized it needed to network innovation ecosystems "to ramp up its efforts in the area of sustainable development" (Altman et al. 2020). Now UNDP "Accelerator Labs interact with businesses, local governments, citizens, schools and universities, other NGOs, and their local UNDP offices to accomplish their mission of speeding up learning and execution while also searching for, creating, and sharing new solutions" (Altman et al. 2020). It is easy to see how this challenge presented itself as an opportunity for "big-thinking." Sustainable development is a massive challenge.

This brings me back to the systematic unifying lens of the *Pattern of Disruptions* to view innovations across customers' expectations to tap into future customers' expectations. "Perhaps one of most difficult aspects of executing a network-of-ecosystems approach is learning from local solutions, generalizing them, and then (where appropriate) relocalizing them for other geographies" (Altman et al. 2020). A universal vantage can help companies translate what they see in a local customer group to trends in other regions. Horizon-scanning and scenario-thinking methodologies will help the most innovative companies to develop new technologies, business models, ecosystems, and organizational competencies for the *Pattern of Disruptions* (see Appendix). The insights in this book give companies an advantage when working in a larger innovation ecosystem, and that is flexibility to orchestrate maneuvers they need "to strike a balance where it leverages just enough capabilities to gain an advantage versus other competitors, but not so many capabilities that by definition its ability to do something new is constrained" (Anthony et al. 2017).

Key Takeaways From Chapter 7

- Resources exist to support the various ways a company wants to deploy open innovation and collaborators.
- Open innovation platforms are a starting place to identify, to connect, and to collaborate across a community of experts.
- Understand the benefits of a partnership by mapping the positions of external partners and the company.
- Continually revisit assumptions to ensure the conditions for decisions reached have not changed.
- Networked innovation ecosystems are the future of disruptive innovation enabled through digital transformation.
- *Part 4: It's Control* is complete.

PART V

Epilogue

Resources

This book is not for "innovation-theater", meaning it is not to enter-
tain readers with euphoric anecdotes to inspire them to be creative.
I wrote this book with the intentions to advance innovation leadership.
This book is for serious executives, business leaders, innovators, and digital marketers intent on growing in the 21st-century. It was important
to me to reflect this dynamic environment, which requires business acumen in new areas of expertise in order to build talent, capabilities, and
resources. Therefore, I packed it with substantive research to prove the
robustness of *Disruptive Innovation Customers' Expectations (DICE)* theory
to tackle complexities that are only visible by combining knowledge across
disruptive innovation and digital transformation. I gathered business
references, case studies, and product examples to demonstrate that
DICE applies across industries, markets, and sectors. *DICE* is relevant
for digital-natives, traditional legacy businesses, incumbents, and new
entrants. I would like to 'Thank' these companies (alphabetical order)
that shared their insights in public works to enable my research: Amazon,
Apple, Duke Energy, Magna Seating, Microsoft, Netflix, Procter and
Gamble, Siemens, Volkswagen, and Walmart.

I built on and evolved the works of others to equip leaders with
dynamic decision-making tools to help position companies for the present
and the future. I believe in the value of knowledge sharing, thought-
leadership, and collaborative-learning. After all, I would not have delivered the insights I shared with you in this book without others publicly
sharing their knowledge. I recognize the value in the phrase: "rising tides
floats all boats." I hope my insights and investments in synthesizing and
organizing the contents in this book evolved the collective practices of
innovation and digital. It is my contribution to leaders around the world,
looking for the right lenses to filter markets, giving order to complexity, and making disruptive innovation simpler. I would like to 'Thank'
Clayton Christensen, Larry Downes, David Rogers, MIT Sloan Research
Team of Andrew A. King and Baljir Baatartogtokh, *Deloitte University*

Press, and interviews conducted by *MIT Sloan Management Review* and *Harvard Business Review*, as well as business case authors.

This book is not the final analysis on disruptive innovation and digital transformation. New developments across all of the topics addressed in this book are subject to evolutionary changes. I am keenly aware that there are unforeseen challenges before leaders, resulting from a multitude of factors, diverging and converging, creating complex environments. Consequently, I included my framework for operationalizing foresight and visioning in the *Appendix: Horizon-Scanning and Scenario-Thinking*. I covered a lot of ground in this book. So here is a recap of the Key Takeaways. You can use this list to trigger thoughts and references back to the parts in the book.

Part 1: It's the Background:

- Christensen's original theory was a first step in alerting incumbents to changing market conditions that threatened their leadership in existing B2B markets.
- Christensen missed a key warning to incumbents: the source of the threats to market leadership is changing consumer behaviors (based on major categories of customers' expectations for value creation, *Pattern of Disruptions*) that include digitally enabled products, services, and business models.
- Digital transformation is a set of capabilities that businesses must develop, which integrates digital to increase value to customers.
- *Pattern of Disruptions* is a guide for innovators and strategists to develop disruptive innovations.
- In addition to the value generation guidance in the pattern, business leaders can leverage maneuvers in the innovation S curve.
- The ability to disrupt across all dimensions in the *DICE Theory* requires ambidextrous leadership.

Part 2: It's the Framework:

- There are three popular models of disruptive innovation, as well as another set of guidelines for a different set of nine patterns of disruption. They use performance as determinants of value creation for disruptive innovation. *DICE* focuses on customers' expectations for value creation.

- The *DICE* model is robust and comprehensive: descriptive, prescriptive, and predictive.
- *DICE* is a complex model with three dimensions: two dimensions captured in the *Pattern of Disruptions* (products/ services and business models), and the third dimension is an innovation S curve that governs saturation levels. Combined these dimensions create interactions and choices for companies with deep understandings of disruptive innovation and digital capabilities.
- The *DICE* model illustrates a dynamic environment for business leaders to navigate and to maneuver. It cautions against prioritizing business model innovations with products/services that are experiencing disruptive innovations, which are redefining customers' expectations, value creation, and purchasing behaviors.
- The work of outcome-driven innovations (job mapping, process maps, observations, segmentation, and mimicking) can be optimized through the *DICE Theory*.
- *DICE* helps companies reinterpret existing sustaining business strategy frameworks and repurpose established R&D tools.
- *DICE* maps out the market entry points along with the strategic choices.
- *DICE* describes the innovation S curve, saturation level, and potential maneuvers.
- The *Pattern of Disruptions* is powerful. It can identify the starting point for the next category of customers' expectations ripe for innovations and can identify the likely places where disruptions can happen next. As companies learn from customers' expectations at each disrupter, it informs their tactics and methods.

Part 3: It's Mastery:

- A customer analysis method is key to data strategy.
- The *Pattern of Disruptions* addresses shortcomings found by industry experts in the popular "Job-to-be-done Approach"

(based on an assessment of customer analysis methods) to help companies identify the types of information, data, and insights needed to have an effective data strategy.

- *DICE* informs data acquisition strategies to empower digital transformation.
- Digital transformation unlocks the value in the digital disrupters in *DICE*: reliable, usable, delightful, and meaningfulness.
- Digital transformation requires companies to engage with customers in new ways. "Big data" will continue to be a challenge for companies looking to build customer loyalty—particularly the vast amounts of data and the various methods customers use to self-select.
- Environments can develop connections that companies need in digital customer acquisitions to invite consumers to "start joining" its loyalty loop without a purchase.
- These three lessons apply to the digital transformation of a physical business: #1: The substance is the same; #2: Just add technology will not work; and #3: Don't forget the user experience.
- A key benefit of disruptive innovation and digital transformation are their abilities to create "first-mover advantage" in a variety of circumstances—just beware of being overconfident.
- Companies that master the techniques and methods in *DICE* are in the best position to play by the new digital rules for businesses enabled with digital capabilities.
- Digitizing business processes and methods without a keen focus on new growth will limit a company's strategic choices and shrink its opportunities to maneuver within the innovation S curve (talent, capabilities, and competitors).
- Building digital capabilities outside of an emphasis on customers is a waste of time.

Part 4: It's Control:

- Accelerate with strategic clarity in terms that everyone understands.

- To reach disruptive innovation in the *Innovation Growth Maturity Framework* start by acknowledging where a company currently resides along the spectrum of capabilities.
- Best practices can be leveraged across an organization for all types of innovation.
- Breakthrough adjacencies unlock pathways to new growth in between core innovations and transformational innovations.
- Digital unlocks new business model innovations.
- Resources exist to support the various ways a company wants to deploy open innovation and collaborators.
- Open innovation platforms are a starting place to identify, to connect, and to collaborate across a community of experts.
- Understand the benefits of a partnership by mapping the positions of external partners and the company.
- Continually revisit assumptions to ensure the conditions for decisions reached have not changed.
- Networked innovation ecosystems are the future of disruptive innovation enabled through digital transformation.

Future Leaders

I apologize for excluding topics on talent, leadership development, organizational change, and company structure. There were not enough opportunities in the book to diverge into these topics, and I did not want to risk minimizing them. Following are a few technology relevant books I recommend for these topics:

- Perez-Breva, Luis. Innovating: a Doer's Manifesto for Starting from a Hunch, Prototyping Problems, Scaling up, and Learning to Be Productively Wrong. MIT Press, 2018.
- Kane, Gerald C., et al. The Technology Fallacy: How People Are the Real Key to Digital Transformation. The MIT Press, 2019.
- Dyer, Jeff, et al. Innovator's DNA, Updated, with a New Preface: Mastering the Five Skills of Disruptive Innovators. Harvard Business Review, 2019.

There are several international universities offering executive leadership and education programs backed by certifications, MBA and Master's degrees focused on digital transformation. Following is a short-list; I am certain that there are others.

- MIT Sloan's Digital Business Strategy Certification courses
- Harvard Business School Digital Transformation Executive Education
- Columbia Business School's Digital Business Leadership Program
- London Business School Digital Transformation and Innovation courses
- HEC Paris Executive Certification, Leading Digital Transformation
- Frankfurt University's Goethe Business School, Master of Digital Transformation Management (MBA)

This book is the first to my knowledge to reveal insights at the intersection of disruptive innovation and digital transformation. It is the result of my professional background in innovation, digital, business, operations, and strategy. If you read my biography you might wonder how a person with my profile came to write a book on this topic. The answers are: research and perspective. I give most of the credit to my Liberal Arts undergraduate education at The College of Wooster, Ohio USA. It instilled in me the value of being a curious learner, the abilities to learn in a variety of ways and in different environments, and synthesize knowledge to extract new meanings. The required intense Independent Study research and writing projects also helped. I share this aspect of my background to challenge leaders to uncover talents within their organizations across the spectrum of academic, training, and experience to build innovation expertise. I invite readers to share their stories of using this book in online reviews, social media platforms, and case studies.

APPENDIX

Horizon-Scanning and Scenario-Thinking

Leaders must be diligent about scanning the edges of markets, across macro and micro vantage points to detect weak signals (megatrends) to stronger signals (actionable outcomes). Numerous business cases detail the missed signals by major companies that led to their eventual demise. So there is no need for this book to placate leaders by softening the message. In fact, I repeatedly stated the price of postponing digital transformation could be extinction and missing a disrupter in the *Pattern of Disruptions* could stall large incumbents. Even without the threat of gloom and doom, setting an actionable vision for scanning and screening opportunity areas is simply good business acumen.

Disruptive innovation requires scanning for threats and opportunities. It commands the attention of senior leadership teams and contributions made from the entire organization. To that end, scouting resources must be mobilized to scan and to sense signals. Since 1995, Mary Meeker, expertly called the "Queen of the Internet," has scanned technology trends and produced the *Internet Trends* report (Clark 2019). There are other companies selling signal services to track signals from the Internet and to monitor technologies, applications, and markets.

Amy Webb, "a quantitative futurist," whose job it is to "investigate the future using data-driven models," has this advice for companies seeking to view the future through traditional linear timelines:

> Teams that rely on traditional linear timelines get caught in a cycle of tactical responses to what feels like constant change being foisted upon them from outside forces. Over time, those tactical responses—which take significant internal alignment and effort—drain the organization's resources and make them vulnerable to disruption. (Webb 2019)

Webb draws an example from her experience consulting with a large tele-communications company on detecting threats. The client chose a 3-year horizon to detect competition in a specific area of wireless communications and ignored scanning for adjacencies. "It was a narrow vision that would take the company down a singular path focused only on streaming and consumer gadgets without considering other disruptive forces on the horizon" (Webb 2020). I try to mitigate these side effects by offering frameworks that operationalize information, making it actionable intelligence despite the time horizon. It is understandable why companies rely on traditional linear timelines. Strategic planning cycles are in 5-year forecasts. The finite timeframe makes it easier to filter, to track, and to confine information. There is more near-term conceivable data and information within a shorter horizon. It is easier to communicate in a systematic way. Timelines compress information to avoid mental overload.

Throughout this book, I shared a myriad of lens (descriptive, prescriptive, and predictive) to leverage the *Pattern of Disruptions*. Also, I recommended supplemental tools and methods to increase the robustness of these views (e.g., models, analysis, frameworks, innovation S curve maneuvers, portfolio strategy for breakthrough adjacencies, and attracting consumers with environments). Horizon-scanning is another framework to improve outcome-driven innovations. If leadership teams do not have a methodology for making actionable predictions about the future then I cover a few frameworks, as well as my own frameworks to offer inspiration:

- "A Futurist's Framework for Strategic Planning," a section from Amy Webb's article, "How to Do Strategic Planning Like a Futurist" (2019). Webb developed "a cone-shaped-framework that measures certainty and charts actions, rather than simply marking the passage of time as quarters or years" (Webb 2019):
  - Step 1: Section the cone into horizons:
    - Tactics (1 to 2 years): the time increment (12 to 24 months) is based on the likelihood that probable events, data, and evidence will be available both inside and outside of the company (Webb 2019);

- Strategy (2 to 5 years): the traditional timeframe when companies revisit their strategies to plan, "defining priorities, allocating resources, and making any personnel changes needed" (Webb 2019);
- Vision (5 to 10 years): making inferences based on possible scenarios "what if" (I explain more about scenarios in the next section); and
- System-level evolution (10+ years): "Leaders can articulate a strong vision for 10 to 15 years in the future while being open to iterating on the strategy and tactic categories as they encounter new tech trends, global events, social changes, and economic shifts" (Webb 2019).
  - Step 2: Identify information sources for the cone's horizons "using highly probable events for which there's already data or evidence, then work outward" (Webb 2019).
- "Creating An Actionable Vision," a chapter from Mark W. Johnson and Josh Suskewicz's book, *Lead from the Future* (2020). A task list that emphasizes key principles in dialogue with senior leaders:
  - Step 1: "explore what the future is likely to hold, targeting the right time horizon" (Johnson et al. 2020);
  - Step 2: apply the implications from step 1, "developing a high-level view of what your customers will value and how market dynamics will work, characterizing the major threats and opportunities that are likely to emerge, and assessing where business-as-usual would likely lead" (Johnson et al. 2020); and
  - Step 3: "assert a point of view on how to best respond to and shape that future, defining the desired future state of your enterprise inclusive of both evolution of its current businesses and the development of new ones" (Johnson et al. 2020).
- My own frameworks, "Horizon-Scanning to Operationalize Visioning" for megatrends and for breakthrough innovations. They are top-down and bottom-up approaches—directionally

focused—to recalibrate actionable strategic plans with dynamic market conditions, avoiding rigid arbitrary parameters.

[T]here is a big difference between [quantitative approaches] trying to predict the future by extrapolating past trends and using intuition to gain insights. Organisations will always use forecasts (effectively predictions) because they need them in order to project sales, create budgets and allocate resources. But to rely on forecasting techniques alone is to flirt with danger. (The *Centre for Strategic Business Studies 1999*)

- ° Steps 1 and 2: Horizon-Scanning to Operationalize Visioning **for Megatrends** are identical to Amy Webb's "A Futurist's Framework for Strategic Planning" with some key exceptions that operationalize the framework.
  - Top-down: Companies can make discussions more real and market driven by tracking by time horizons, focusing on "Tactics (1 to 2 years)," which could be new pricing, new supplier, incremental products; "Strategy (2 to 5 years)," which could be new products, adjacencies, digital platforms, new services, or new user experience; "Vision (5 to 10 years)," which could be acquisitions, new business models, transformational technologies; and "System-level evolution (10+ years)" which could be the development of a new innovation ecosystem or value chain to support transformational products.
  - Bottom-up: Companies can make outcomes more actionable by tracking factors as they progress beginning with market and technology trends, to new applications, to new markets, to new customers, and lastly to new product specifications.
- ° Steps 1 and 2: Horizon-Scanning to Operationalize Visioning **for Breakthrough Innovations**.

- Top-down: The time horizons are the same as the previous framework for megatrends.
- Bottom-up: The actionable outcomes are core adjacency, platform adjacency, radical adjacency, and multisided platform.
  ○ Step 3: Use both frameworks to discuss with leadership teams (use a table format). See Chapter 6 for the steps on Horizon-Scanning to Operationalize Visioning **for Breakthrough Innovations**. See Table A.1 for sample formatting of Horizon-Scanning to Operationalize Visioning **for Megatrends**:
    - Elements for "top-down approach": (column headings in time horizon order).
    - Elements for "bottom-up approach": (row headings in action order).
    - In each cell document the outside and inside worlds for each column/row. Take information from scouting reports (e.g., technologies and market developments), sensing from internal sales, customer service, technicians and repair personnel, and input from strategic customers and suppliers.
    - On occasion, I share individual frameworks with strategic customers, ecosystem partners, and suppliers to assess a vision-match for the future and to begin collaboration discussions or to guide open innovation efforts, including cocreation agreements.
    - I annually schedule releases (or more frequently depending on dynamic changes in the landscape on a quarterly basis); one or two frameworks will be updated and shared with the entire leadership organization to discern distribution within their teams.

In contrast to the time horizon approach of the above foresight frameworks, scenario-thinking is more narrowly focused on a specific challenge. I find scenario-thinking works best in project teams where the

Table A.1 *Horizon-scanning to operationalize visioning (sample format)*

è Input information across all horizons"	Tactical (1–2 years)	Strategy (2–5 years)	Vision (5–10 years)	System-level evolution (10+ years)
Market trends	Example: new pricing, new supplier, incremental products	Example: new products, digital platforms, service, user experiences	Example: acquisition, new business models, transformational technology	Example: new ecosystem or value chain to support transformational products
Technology trends				
New applications				
New markets				
New customers				
New product specifications				

challenge is within the Vision (5 to 10 years) horizon, for example, business model innovations and new technologies. "So, at the intuitive end of the spectrum lies another tool: scenarios" (*CSBS* 1999). This is where both intuition and forecast are needed. There is a 50/50 split between "knowns" (within the five-year horizon) and "unknowns" (in another five-year time). "The gravest risk is that forecasts tend to project conventional wisdom and current assumptions forward. They fit well with existing mindsets" (*CSBS* 1999).

The objective of scenario-thinking is not to prove one methodology more right than others. It is to recognize that assumptions are the fundamental culprits that need to be exposed based on actual events developing in reality. There are three categories or types of methodologies for scenarios (in order of simplest to hardest):

1. *Intuitive logic* is imaginative (*CSBS* 1999). It challenges the mindsets of managers to think in different contexts and under certain conditions of a reality that may be based on facts but could also require some imagination. Storytelling is an effective tool for this "soft" method of scenario development.

2. *Trend-impact analysis* is quantitative. It relies on trend analysis over time to predict the direction or the inflection points to watch out for the probabilities of a set of conditions happening because of "one key decision or forecast variable which is quantitative and on which

historical information exists" (*CSBS* 1999), for example, commodity supply chain shortages or political elections.

3. *Cross-impact analysis* is qualitative. It is a calculated matrix of variables based on experts, "identifying a large number of trends, potential events and conditions, which may affect the likelihood of other events occurring" (*CSBS* 1999) to create scenarios—each scenario receives a probability. There is software to calculate and to plot the different combinations.

References

Adobe, C.M.O. 2018. "Forrester Consulting: It Pays To Be An Experience-Led Business." In *CMO.Adobe.Com, Forrester Consulting.* cmo.adobe. com/articles/2018/4/forrester-consulting-it-pays-to-be-an-experience-led-business.html#gs.8568me.

Afshar, V. 2019. "New Customer Expectations Are Rewriting the Digital Transformation Playbook." *ZDNet,* www.zdnet.com/article/rewriting-the-digital-transformation-playbook/

Altman, E.J., and F. Nagle. 2020. "Accelerating Innovation Through a Network of Ecosystems." *MIT Sloan Management Review,* sloanreview.mit.edu/article/accelerating-innovation/

Anderson, J.C., and A.N. James. 2014. "Business Marketing: Understand What Customers Value." *Harvard Business Review,* hbr.org/1998/11/business-marketing-understand-what-customers-value

Anthony, S.D., M. Johnson, and J. Sinfield. 2008. "The Innovator's Guide to Growth: Putting Disruptive Innovation to Work." *Harvard Business Review.*

Beasley, D. 2020. " Google Parent Drops "Smart City" Project In Toronto." *Forbes Magazine,* www.forbes.com/sites/beasleydavid/2020/05/08/google-parent-drops-smart-city-project-in-toronto/#64da1b3a5f65

Bessen, J. 2014. "Industrial Revolution Lessons for Today's Age of Open Innovation." *Slate Magazine,* slate.com/technology/2014/05/william-gilmour-power-loom-the-industrial-revolution-and-open-innovation.html

Bettencourt, L., and W.U. Anthony. 2015. " The Customer-Centered Innovation Map." *Harvard Business Review,* hbr.org/2008/05/the-customer-centered-innovation-map?autocomplete=true

Bower, J.L., and C.M. Christensen,. 1995. "Disruptive Technologies: Catching the Wave." *Harvard Business Review* https://hbr.org/1995/01/disruptive-technologies-catching-the-wave

Buchanan, L., and J.S. Carolyn. 2007. "Motorola and the RAZR." *Thunderbird School of Management* , Vol. TB007, pp. 1–8.

Bucic, T., and S. Gaganpreet. 2018. "Apple Watch: Managing Innovation Resistance." *Ivey Business School Foundation*

Bughin, J., and N. Zeebroeck. 2017. "MIT Sloan Management Review's The Best Response to Digital Disruption." *McKinsey & Company,* www.mckinsey.com/mgi/overview/in-the-news/the-right-response-to-digital-disruption

Brown, B., and S.D. Anthony. 2017. "How P&G Tripled Its Innovation Success Rate." *Harvard Business Review*, hbr.org/2011/06/how-pg-tripled-its-innovation-success-rate

Cancialosi, C. 2017. "Why Culture Is The Heart Of Organizational Innovation." *Forbes Magazine*, www.forbes.com/sites/chriscancialosi/2017/02/07/why-culture-is-the-heart-of-organizational-innovation/#27613e153f4d

"Chapter 3: Creating An Inspiring And Actionable Vision.' Lead from the Future: How to Turn Visionary Thinking into Breakthrough Growth, by Mark W." 2020. *Johnson and Josh Suskewicz, Harvard Business Review Press*, pp. 75–99.

Christensen, C.M., and M.E. Raynor. 2003. *Why Hard-Nosed Executives Should Care about Management Theory. Harvard Business Review*, Vol. 81. https://ncbi.nlm.nih.gov/pubmed/12964394

Christensen, C.M. 2016. *Competing Against Luck: The Story of Innovation and Customer Choice*. HarperBusiness, an Imprint of HarperCollins Publishers.

Christensen, C.M., M.W. Johnson, K. Darrell, and Rigby. 2002. "Foundations for Growth: How to Identify and Build Disruptive New Businesses." *MIT Sloan Management Review*.

Christensen, C.M. 2016. "The Innovator's Dilemma: When New Technologies Cause Great Firms to Fail." *Harvard Business Review*.

Christensen, C.M., E.R. Michael, and R. McDonald. 2016. "The Ubiquitous "Disruptive Innovation."" *Harvard Business Review*.

Christensen, C.M. 2020. "What Is Disruptive Innovation?" *Harvard Business Review*, hbr.org/2015/12/what-is-disruptive-innovation

Clark, K. 2019. "Here's Mary Meeker's 2019 Internet Trends Report." *TechCrunch*, techcrunch.com/2019/06/11/internet-trends-report-2019/

Innovation, C. 1994. "Procter & Gamble: Swiffer. We Still Pushed a__heavy Bucket and Rag Mop__around the House, Watching the Soapy Water Turn Dark with Dirt Well before the Job Was Done." Continuum Innovation.

Corkindale, G. 2014. "In Praise of Brilliant Failure." *Harvard Business Review*, July, hbr.org/2007/06/in-praise-of-brilliant-failure

Crandell, C. 2016. "Customer Co-Creation Is The Secret Sauce To Success." *Forbes Magazine*, www.forbes.com/sites/christinecrandell/2016/06/10/customer_cocreation_secret_sauce/#76f2b3955b6d

Danziger, P.N. 2018. "Walmart Doubles Down On Its Transformation Into A Technology Company." *Forbes Magazine*, www.forbes.com/sites/pamdanziger/2018/10/22/walmart-doubles-down-on-its-transformation-into-a-technology-company/#58d22abe404c

Jong, Marc, and M. Dijk. 2015. "Disrupting Beliefs: A New Approach to Business-Model Innovation." *McKinsey & Company*, www.mckinsey.com/business-functions/strategy-and-corporate-finance/our-insights/disrupting-beliefs-a-new-approach-to-business-model-innovation

Debter, L. 2019. "Amazon Surpasses Walmart As The World's Largest Retailer." *Forbes Magazine*, www.forbes.com/sites/laurendebter/2019/05/15/worlds-largest-retailers-2019-amazon-walmart-alibaba/#264ffcfd4171

Deloitte. 2015. "Pattern of Disruptions." *Deloitte Consulting LLP's Strategy & Operations*. Deloitte University Press.

"Disruptive Shock Waves and Dual Transformation.' Dual Transformation How to Reposition Today's Business While Creating the Future, by Scott D. Anthony et Al." 2017. *Harvard Business Review Press*, 1–24.

Downes, L., and P. Nunes. 2015. *Big Bang Disruption: Business Survival in the Age of Constant Innovation*. Portfolio Penguin.

Economist. 2020. "Should Data Be Crunched at the Centre or at the Edge?' The Economist." *The Economist Newspape*, www.economist.com/special-report/2020/02/20/should-data-be-crunched-at-the-centre-or-at-the-edge

Economist. 2020. "Governments Are Erecting Borders for Data." *The Economist Newspaper*, www.economist.com/special-report/2020/02/20/governments-are-erecting-borders-for-data

Edelman, D.C. 2016. "Branding in the Digital Age: You're Spending Your Money in All the Wrong Places." *Harvard Business Review*, hbr.org/2010/12/branding-in-the-digital-age-youre-spending-your-money-in-all-the-wrong-places

Edelman, D.C., and M. Singer. 2016. "Competing on Customer Journeys." *Harvard Business Review*, hbr.org/2015/11/competing-on-customer-journeys

Fockenbrock, D. 2019. "Expensive Fleet: The Car Sharing Flop from Daimler and BMW." *Handelsblatt.Com, Handelsblatt.Com*, www.handelsblatt.com/unternehmen/industrie/mobilitaetsdienste-teure-flotte-der-carsharing-flop-von-daimler-und-bmw/v_detail_tab_p

Forsgren, R. 2019. "Dieselgate: A Case Study in Engineering Ethics." *National Aeronautics and Space Administration*.

Furr, N., and A. Shipilov. 2020. "Digital Doesn't Have to Be Disruptive." *Harvard Business Review*, hbr.org/2019/07/digital-doesnt-have-to-be-disruptive

Garcia, T. 2019. "Walmart's Digital Efforts Paying off in Battle with Amazon." *MarketWatch*, www.marketwatch.com/story/walmart-is-snapping-up-e-commerce-market-share-from-amazon-2019-05-16

Gartner_Inc. n.d. "Hype Cycle." https://gartner.com/en/information-technology/glossary/hype-cycle

Gartnercom. 2020. "The Edge Completes the Cloud: A Gartner Trend Insight Report." *Gartner.Com*, www.gartner.com/en/doc/3889058-the-edge-completes-the-cloud-a-gartner-trend-insight-report

Good, L.J., and P. Michelman. 2017. "Leading in a Time of Increased Expectations." *MIT Sloan Management Review*, sloanreview.mit.edu/article/leading-in-a-time-of-increased-expectations/

Green, A. 2020. "Complete Guide to Privacy Laws in the US: Varonis." *Inside Out Security*, www.varonis.com/blog/us-privacy-laws/#:~:text=US%20Privacy%20Laws,alone%20a%20data%20security%20law.&text=In%20brief%2C%20both%20the%20CCPA,of%20processing%20at%20any%20time

Greene, T. 2020. *"What Is the Internet Backbone and How It Works."* Network World, Network World. www.networkworld.com/article/3532318/what-is-the-internet-backbone-and-how-it-works.html

Greiner, A. 2018. "A History of Lyft, from Fuzzy Pink Mustaches to Global Ride Share Giant." *CNN, Cable News Network*, www.cnn.com/interactive/2019/03/business/lyft-history/index.html

Grove, H. 2018. "Selling Solutions Isn't Enough." *MIT Sloan Management Review*, sloanreview.mit.edu/article/selling-solutions-isnt-enough/

Habibi, A. 2014. "Delphi Technique Theoretical Framework in Qualitative Research." *The International Journal of Engineering and Science* 3, no. 4, pp. 8–13. https://doi.org/10.9790/1813-060502.

Hagiu, A., and J. Wright. 2019. "When Data Creates Competitive Advantage." *Harvard Business Review*, hbr.org/2020/01/when-data-creates-competitive-advantage

Hagiu, A., and J.A. Elizabeth. 2017. "Is There a Platform in Your Product?" *Harvard Business Review*, hbr.org/2017/07/finding-the-platform-in-your-product

Hagiu, A. 2013. "Strategic Decisions for Multisided Platforms." *MIT Sloan Management Review*, sloanreview.mit.edu/article/strategic-decisions-for-multisided-platforms/

Historycom, ed. 2009. "Ford's Assembly Line Starts Rolling." In *History.Com, A&E Television Networks*, www.history.com/this-day-in-history/fords-assembly-line-starts-rolling

Horn, M.B. 2017. "Disruptive Innovations." *Christensen Institute*. https://christenseninstitute.org/disruptive-innovations/.

Huston, L., and N. Sakkab. n.d. "Connect and Develop: Inside Procter & Gamble's New Model for Innovation." *Harvard Business Review*.

Jefferies, D. 2019. "Disruptive Innovation: What Is It and Why Don't Leaders 'Get' It?" Raconteur. Raconteur Media Ltd.

Jr, Tom Huddleston. 2014. "Google, Verizon Could Help NYC Turn Pay-Phones into WiFi Hotspots." *Fortune*, July, fortune..

Johnson, M.W. 2018. "Reinvent Your Business Model: How to Seize the White Space for Transformative Growth." *Harvard Business Review Press*.

Kane, G.C. 2017. "Digital Disruption Is a People Problem." *MIT Sloan Management Review*, sloanreview.mit.edu/article/digital-disruption-is-a-people-problem/

Kane, G.C. 2018. "Why Companies Don't Respond to Digital Disruption." *MIT Sloan Management Review*, sloanreview.mit.edu/article/why-companies-dont-respond-to-digital-disruption/

Kiesnoski, K. 2017. "The Top 10 US Companies by Market Capitalization." In *CNBC*, www.cnbc.com/2017/03/08/the-top-10-us-companies-by-market-capitalization.html

Kim, W.C., and M. Renée. 2005. *Blue Ocean Strategy*. Harvard Business School Press.

King, A.A., and B. Baatartogtokh. 2015. "How Useful Is the Theory of Disruptive Innovation?" *MIT Sloan Management Review, MIT Sloan Management Review*, sloanreview.mit.edu/article/how-useful-is-the-theory-of-disruptive-innovation/

Kirby, J., and A.S. Thomas. 2014. "The Institutional Yes." *Harvard Business Review, Harvard Business Review*, hbr.org/2007/10/the-institutional-yes

Iansiti, M., and K.R. Lakhani. n.d. "Competing in the Age of AI." *Harvard Business Review*. hbr.org/2020/01/competing-in-the-age-of-ai

Idelchik, M., and S. Kogan. 2015. "GE's Open Collaboration Model." Taylor and Francis Online, Research Technology Management. https://doi.org/10.5437/08956308X5504101

iRobot. 2020. *"IRobot® Braava Jet® M6."* IRobot, IRobot. store.irobot.com/default/floor-mopping-braava-robot-mop-irobot-braava-jet-m6/m611020.html?gclid=EAIaIQobChMImeKbkp3c6QIVCdbACh1ElQLGEAQYASABEgJeIPD_BwE&gclsrc=aw.ds

Lafley, A.G., and L.M. Roger. 2013. "Playing to Win: How Strategy Really Works." *Harvard Business Review Press*.

Lambert, D.M., and G.E. Matias. 2020. "Co-Creating Value: The next Level in Customer-Supplier Relationships." *CSCMP's Supply Chain Quarterly*, www.supplychainquarterly.com/articles/1047-co-creating-value-the-next-level-in-customer-supplier-relationships

MaayanJanMaayan, J., and G. David. 2020. "The IoT Rundown For 2020: Stats, Risks, and Solutions." *Security Today*, securitytoday.com/articles/2020/01/13/the-iot-rundown-for-2020.aspx#gsc.tab=0

Madehowcom. 2020. "Mop." *How Products Are Made*. Advameg, Inc. www.madehow.com/Volume-7/Mop.html

Madgavkar, A. 2019. "The Tougher Competitors in Emerging Markets." *McKinsey & Company*, www.mckinsey.com/business-functions/strategy-and-corporate-finance/our-insights/the-tougher-competitors-in-emerging-markets

Seating, M. 2018. "News Release - Magna Reveals New Seating Ecosystem Designed to Offer More Flexible, Collaborative Interior." www.magna.com/company/newsroom/releases/release/2018/12/10/news-release---magna-reveals-new-seating-ecosystem-designed-to-offer-more-flexible-collaborative-interior

McAfee, A., and E. Brynjolfsson. 2018. *Machine, Platform, Crowd: Harnessing Our Digital Future.* W W Norton.

McDonald, R., and K.M. Eisenhardt. 2020. "The New-Market Conundrum." *Harvard Business Review*, hbr.org/2020/05/the-new-market-conundrum

McGrath, R.G., and R. McManus. 2020. "Discovery-Driven Digital Transformation." *Harvard Business Review*, hbr.org/2020/05/discovery-driven-digital-transformation

McGrath, R.G. 2019. *Seeing around Corners: How to Spot Inflection Points in Business before They Happen.* Houghton Mifflin Harcourt.

Merge, n. 2016. "On Strategy and Innovation." In *NMerge, NMerge Https://Secure.Gravatar.Com/Avatar/Ce0755d38d6244f0bf5581a7e16f 5bb1?S=96&D=Mm&R=g*, www.nmerge.com/strategy-and-innovation/

Meyersohn, N. 2018. "There Are Still 100,000 Pay Phones in America." *CNNMoney, Cable News Network*, money.cnn.com/2018/03/19/news/companies/pay-phones/index.html

Mintzberg, H., and J. Lampel. 1999. "Reflecting on the Strategy Process." *MIT Sloan Management Review*, sloanreview.mit.edu/article/reflecting-on-the-strategy-process/

Moazed, A., and L.J. Nicholas. 2016. "Why Clayton Christensen Is Wrong About Uber And Disruptive Innovation." *TechCrunch*, https://techcrunch.com/2016/02/27/why-clayton-christensen-is-wrong-about-uber-and-disruptive-innovation/

Moin, D. 2016. "J. Crew Gets Active with New Balance." *Los Angeles Times*, www.latimes.com/fashion/la-ig-fashion-jcrew-new-balance-active-wear20161011-snap-story.html

Moore, G.A. 2014. *Crossing the Chasm Marketing and Selling Disruptive Products to Mainstream Customers.* Harper Business.

Morgan, B. 2019. "100 Stats On Digital Transformation And Customer Experience." *Forbes Magazine* www.forbes.com/sites/blakemorgan/2019/12/16/100-stats-on-digital-transformation-and-customer-experience/#5abccfd03bf3

Murnane, K. 2020. "There Is No Console War Because Xbox Moved On And Left PlayStation Behind." *Forbes Magazine*, February, www.forbes.com/sites/kevinmurnane/2020/02/09/there-is-no-console-war-because-xbox-moved-on-and-left-playstation-behind/#6008e19674c2

Nagji, B., and T. Geoff. 2015. "Managing Your Innovation Portfolio." *Harvard Business Review*, hbr.org/2012/05/managing-your-innovation-portfolio

Nicas, J. 2018. "Apple Is Worth $1,000,000,000,000. Two Decades Ago, It Was Almost Bankrupt." *The New York Times*, www.nytimes.com/2018/08/02/technology/apple-stock-1-trillion-market-cap.html

Nunes, P., and T. Breene. 2011. *Jumping the S Curve: How Great Companies Get on Top and Stay There.* Harvard Business.

Nunes, P., and T. Breene. 2019. "Reinvent Your Business Before It's Too Late." *Harvard Business Review*, hbr.org/2011/01/reinvent-your-business-before-its-too-late

Ozkan, N.N. 2015. "An Example of Open Innovation: P&G." *Procedia - Social and Behavioral Sciences* 195, pp. 1496–1502. https://doi.org/10.1016/j.sbspro.2015.06.450

Park, H.S. 2017. "Technology Convergence, Open Innovation, and Dynamic Economy." *Journal of Open Innovation: Technology, Market, and Complexity, SpringerOpen*, link.springer.com/article/10.1186/s40852-017-0074-z

Parker, G.G. 2016. *Platform Revolution: How Networked Markets Are Transforming the Economy and How to Make Them… Work for You.* W W Norton.

Porter, M.E. 2015. "How Competitive Forces Shape Strategy." *Harvard Business Review*, hbr.org/1979/03/how-competitive-forces-shape-strategy

Porter, M.E. 2019. "What Is Strategy?" *Harvard Business Review*, November, hbr..

PTCcom. 2020. "Digital Transformation Report by Corporate Leaders and PTC." *PTC*, www.ptc.com/en/products/plm/capabilities/digital-transformation-report

Quesenberry, K.A. 2016. "Fix Your Social Media Strategy by Taking It Back to Basics." *Harvard Business Review*, hbr.org/2016/07/fix-your-social-media-strategy-by-taking-it-back-to-basics

Reinhardt, R., and G. Sebastian. 2011. "Enabling Disruptive Innovations through the Use of Customer Analysis Methods." *Review of Managerial Science* 5, no. 4, pp. 291–307. https://doi.org/10.1007/s11846-011-0069-2.

Ries, E. 2014. *The Lean Startup: How Today's Entrepreneurs Use Continuous Innovation to Create Radically Successful Businesses.* Crown Business.

Rogers, D.L. 2016. *The Digital Transformation Playbook: Rethink Your Business for the Digital Age.* Columbia University Press.

Satell, G. 2018. "The 4 Types of Innovation and the Problems They Solve." *Harvard Business Review*, hbr.org/2017/06/the-4-types-of-innovation-and-the-problems-they-solve

Satell, G. 2014. "Why The Digital Revolution Is Really Just Getting Started." *Forbes Magazine*, www.forbes.com/sites/gregsatell/2014/04/05/why-the-digital-revolution-is-really-just-getting-started/#be038a23a72c

Seward, Z.M. 2013. "The First Mobile Phone Call Was Made 40 Years Ago Today." *The Atlantic, Atlantic Media Company*, www.theatlantic.com/technology/archive/2013/04/the-first-mobile-phone-call-was-made-40-years-ago-today/274611/

Shaughnessy, H. 2011. "The 10 Most Important Trends in Business." *Forbes, Forbes Magazine*, www.forbes.com/sites/haydnshaughnessy/2011/09/22/the-10-most-important-trends-in-business/#5cf565fe30d2

Siebel, T.M. 2019. "Digital Transformation: Survive and Thrive in an Era of Mass Extinction." *RosettaBooks*.

Siegele, L. 2020. "A Deluge of Data Is Giving Rise to a New Economy." *The Economist Newspaper*, www.economist.com/special-report/2020/02/20/a-deluge-of-data-is-giving-rise-to-a-new-economy

Siegele, L. 2016. "What Is the "Splinternet"?' The Economist." *The Economist Newspaper*, www.economist.com/the-economist-explains/2016/11/22/what-is-the-splinternet

Sutton, R.I. 2014. "Threat ... or Opportunity?" *Harvard Business Review*, hbr.org/2007/06/threat-or-opportunity

"The Centre for Strategie Business Studies (CSBS). 'Scenarios: The Search for Foresight." 1999. *The Antidote*, no. 22, pp. 4–13.

Thompson, N.C. 2020. "Why Innovation's Future Isn't (Just) Open." *MIT Sloan Management Review, MIT Sloan Management Review*, sloanreview.mit.edu/article/why-innovations-future-isnt-just-open/

Tweedie, S. 2015. "The World's First Smartphone, Simon, Was Created 15 Years before the IPhone." *Business Insider, Business Insider*, www.businessinsider.com/worlds-first-smartphone-simon-launched-before-iphone-2015-6

Ucuzoglu, J., and J. Hagel III. 2020. "Use Your Customer Data to Actually Help Your Customers." *Harvard Business Review*, hbr.org/2020/04/use-your-customer-data-to-actually-help-your-customers?ab=hero-main-text

Ulwick, A.W. 2014. "Turn Customer Input into Innovation." *Harvard Business Review*, , hbr.org/2002/01/turn-customer-input-into-innovation

Alstyne, V., and W. Marshall. 2017. "Pipelines, Platforms, and the New Rules of Strategy." *Harvard Business Review*, hbr.org/2016/04/pipelines-platforms-and-the-new-rules-of-strategy

Vangsgaard, C., and G. Martin Nylokke. 2015. "Growing Beyond Your Core." *ReD Associates*, www.redassociates.com/perspectives-posts/2015/10/1/growing-beyond-your-core

Webb, A. 2020. "The 11 Sources of Disruption Every Company Must Monitor." *MIT Sloan Management Review*, sloanreview.mit.edu/article/the-11-sources-of-disruption-every-company-must-monitor/

Webb, A. 2019. "How to Do Strategic Planning Like a Futurist." *Harvard Business Review*, hbr.org/2019/07/how-to-do-strategic-planning-like-a-futurist

Webb, K. 2019. "From the Internet to the IPhone, Here Are the 20 Most Important Inventions of the Last 30 Years." *Business Insider*, www.businessinsider.com/most-important-inventions-of-last-30-years-internet-iphone-netflix-facebook-google-2019-5

World Economic Forum, Editors. 2020. "World Economic Forum,,'Building a Digital Automotive Industry." In *Digital Transformation, World Economic Forum*, reports.weforum.org/digital-transformation/building-a-digital-automotive-industry/

World Economic Forum, Editors. 2015. "The Internet of Things and Connected Devices: Making the World Smarter." In *Digital Transformation, Accenture Digital Consumer Survey*, reports.weforum.org/digital-transformation/the-internet-of-things-and-connected-devices-making-the-world-smarter/

World Economic Forum, Editors. 2019. "Reinventing the Wheel: Digital Transformation in the Automotive Industry." In *Digital Transformation, World Economic Forum*, reports.weforum.org/digital-transformation/reinventing-the-wheel-the-digital-transformation-of-the-automotive-industry/

World Health Organization (WHO). 2009. "World Health Organization." *Bulletin of the World Health Organization* 87, no. 8, pp. 565–644. doi:https://www.who.int/bulletin/volumes/87/8/09-040809/en/#:~:text=Direct%2Dto%2Dconsumer%20advertising%20of,(long%20format%20television%20commercials

Zook, C., and J. Allen. 2014. "Growth Outside the Core." *Harvard Business Review*, hbr.org/2003/12/growth-outside-the-core

About the Author

Marguerite leads transformational innovation growth strategies. Her expertise includes: Disruptive Innovation, Digital Transformation, Ideation, Customer Insights, Digital Marketing, Digital Business Models and Platforms, Open Innovation, Co-Creation, and Innovation Ecosystems.

Marguerite's business leadership and market knowledge extends across many commercial and industrial markets: automotive electrification, vehicle electronic safety systems, engines, heavy off-road equipment, and plastics.

Marguerite earned a Master's degree in Acquisitions Management from Central Michigan University and several professional certifications from Northwestern University, Kellogg, Harvard Business School, and MIT Sloan. She is a twice US Patented Inventor. She is on the Board of Directors for the Innovation Research Interchange (IRI) 2019-2021.

Booking and event information: www.TheNextIsh.com
Connect via LinkedIn: https://linkedin.com/in/margueritejohnson/

Index

OTHER TITLES IN THE SERVICE SYSTEMS AND INNOVATIONS IN BUSINESS AND SOCIETY COLLECTION

Jim Spohrer, IBM & Haluk Demirkan, University of Washington, Editors

- *Build Better Brains* by Martina Muttke
- *Service Excellence in Organizations, Volume II* by Fiona Urquhart
- *Service Excellence in Organizations, Volume I* by Fiona Urquhart
- *Obtaining Value from Big Data for Service Systems, Volume II* by Stephen H. Kaisler, Frank Armour, and Alberto J. Espinosa
- *Obtaining Value from Big Data for Service Systems, Volume I* by Stephen H. Kaisler, Frank Armour, and Alberto J. Espinosa
- *The Value Imperative* by Gautam Mahajan
- *Co-Design, Volume I* by Mark Gatenby, and Stefan Cantore
- *Co-Design, Volume II* by Mark Gatenby
- *Co-Design, Volume III* by Stefan Cantore
- *Everything Old is New Again* by Miriam Plavin-Masterman
- *How Creating Customer Value Makes You a Great Executive* by Gautam Mahajan
- *Sustainability and the City* by Adi Wolfson
- *The Accelerating TechnOnomic Medium ('ATOM')* by Kartik Gada
- *How Can Digital Technologies Improve Public Services and Governance?* by Nagy K. Hanna
- *Collaborative Innovation* by Tony Morgan

Concise and Applied Business Books

The Collection listed above is one of 30 business subject collections that Business Expert Press has grown to make BEP a premiere publisher of print and digital books. Our concise and applied books are for...

- Professionals and Practitioners
- Faculty who adopt our books for courses
- Librarians who know that BEP's Digital Libraries are a unique way to offer students ebooks to download, not restricted with any digital rights management
- Executive Training Course Leaders
- Business Seminar Organizers

Business Expert Press books are for anyone who needs to dig deeper on business ideas, goals, and solutions to everyday problems. Whether one print book, one ebook, or buying a digital library of 110 ebooks, we remain the affordable and smart way to be business smart. For more information, please visit www.businessexpertpress.com, or contact sales@businessexpertpress.com.